PRAISE FOR *YOUR BUT'S TOO BIG*

Travis is an inspiring young leader I've mentored for many years. The insights in this book come out of his deep desire to see you fulfill God's calling for your life. Take the time to apply every powerful and practical step so you can move forward and live God's best for your life.

Rick Warren
Pastor, Saddleback Church
Lake Forest, CA

Excuses are dream killers. Don't trade even the smallest of excuses for your God-sized dreams. If you're ready to live out what God has destined you for, this book is for you. *Your But's Too Big* will light a fire within you to go after your dreams—no more ifs, ands, or buts.

Mark Batterson
New York Times best-selling author of a dozen books,
including *The Circle Maker, All In*, and *If*

This book offers far more than motivation and information—this is a book that delivers transformation. Motivation lasts only a moment; transformation lasts a lifetime. If you're looking for a book that will launch you into living out your God-sized dreams, this is the book for you!

Miles McPherson
Pastor, Rock Church
San Diego, CA

Simply incredible. This book will give you a lifelong injection of spiritual motivation. You will discover the keys that will open the doors for you to live a life of no excuses. This is also the perfect book for me to take my entire church through.

Leo Bigger
Senior Pastor, International Christian Church
Zurich, Switzerland

Wow! This is not just a book to read, but a manual for living. The powerful Bible stories and practical life stories contained within will not only encourage and equip you, they will also catapult you into living out God's purpose for your life. Whether you're about to take a huge leap of faith into living your most audacious dreams or trying to overcome some of life's most challenging obstacles, this book is for you.

Naeem Fazaal
Senior Pastor, Mosaic Church
South Carolina

I love it. Killer title and killer content. There's not a person alive who doesn't need this book. We all make excuses, and this is the perfect book to put them behind us once and for all!

Tim Harlow
Senior Pastor, Parkview Church
Orland Park, Illinois

I wish I would have had a book like this when I was a child. I have personally been through many trials that could have stopped me in my tracks. But because of God's amazing grace and strength, I've been able to rise above! And that is exactly what this book is about. No matter what you've been through or what you're going through,

God has a a plan and purpose for your life. And with God's help, He will see you through. No excuses!

Krystal Thomas
Former Player, WNBA, USA Basketball, Duke University
Assistant Basketball Coach, Grand Canyon University

Such a great read. I have had the privilege to know Travis for the last twelve years as one of my chaplains in the NBA. Every time I come to Phoenix, I look forward to hearing what God has put on his heart for our team. Now, every time he writes, I look forward to reading. This book is perfect for the underdog. For the person, much like myself, who has had to completely depend on God and work tirelessly to achieve every dream. If you're tired of surrendering to excuses, you have to read this book!

Steve Blake
Player, NBA, USA Basketball

Spectacular. This book makes the TOP 10 highlights for must reads for the year. *Your BUT's Too Big* is engaging, encouraging, and equipping. It's loaded with Bible stories and life stories that leap off the page and into the depths of your soul. Travis' easy style of writing comes across as both personal and practical. This isn't just a book; it's a guidebook filled with ingredients to put your excuses behind you once and for all. Go ahead, read it. And begin to live your dreams!

Jason Romano
ESPN Producer

Travis has been inspiring and motivating professional basketball players for well over a decade. He's become a trusted voice for influencing the influencers. Travis possesses a true gift for moving people beyond their fears and failures and into their dreams and desires. This book is compelling, challenging, and refreshingly candid. Whatever might be holding you back from pursuing your God-given dreams, this book is the perfect tool to push you through.

Jerry Colangelo
Chairman, USA Basketball
Chairman, Naismith Memorial Basketball Hall of Fame

Travis is a personal friend and we share many things in common: we both pastor churches, minister to pro athletes, strongly believe in multiethnic churches, and desire to see people live their God-given dream for God's glory. As a former NFL player and current pastor, I'm very familiar with the challenges one faces while pursuing a dream. In this book, Travis does a tremendous job of addressing many of those challenges, while outlining powerful Bible-based solutions to overcome them. *Your BUT's Too Big* is a must read for every athlete, pastor, entrepreneur, and dreamer!

Derwin Grey
Lead Pastor, Transformation Church
Former NFL Player
Author, *Limitless Life* & *The High Definition Leader*

Home run! Travis knocked it out of the park with this one. Becoming a professional baseball player wasn't something that was handed to me on silver platter. I had to work for it tirelessly. I could have easily given up on the dream before I even got started. *Your BUT's Too Big* is a playbook that emphasizes a crucial concept for every dreamer—never quit on something you believe in. If you strike out in life, you gotta get back in the batter's box and keep swinging until one day you knock your dream out of the park! This book is an action plan for believing in a dream *and* achieving it.

Eric Young, Jr.
Player, MLB

Travis is an anointed leader whose commitment to God, leadership, and making an impact in peoples' lives sets him apart. Relatable and inspiring, this book speaks life into your dreams. It is empowering, humorous, and filled with revelation. Travis' insight and leadership will take your life to another level.

Kim Dolan Leto
Author, *F.I.T. Faith Inspired Transformation,* and Speaker

Excellent resource, exceptional content, and exactly what every person needs to read! By the time you're finished reading this book, you will feel like there's nothing you can't do because God is with you. Excuses have the ability to keep you short of the promised land God has for your life. We're all susceptible to the temptation of making excuses, which is why this book is so important. To live a life without excuse—and be *totally* available for God's use!

Danny Gokey
BMG Recording Artist
Founder, Sophia's Heart
Author, *Hope In Front of Me*

Travis Hearn is the real deal. He has personally spoken God's Word into my life throughout the years during countless Bible studies. He is passionate about God and passionate about helping people. This book sums up everything I know about Travis. He desires that each one of us live out God's best for our lives, and nothing less. His words will spark a fire in your soul and elevate your relationship with Christ to a whole new level.

Isaiah Thomas
NBA Player

Travis is my pastor, and my family and I attend Impact Church. God has given him the incredible ability to communicate God's

Word. Whether from the pulpit or from a book, Travis has a way of pushing me in my walk with God to a location that I would have never gone otherwise. When you read this book, you will not only be inspired; you will grow closer to Christ.

Ronnie Price
NBA Player

YOUR
BUT's
TOO BIG!

LEAVING YOUR EXCUSES BEHIND

YOUR
BUT's
TOO BIG!

LEAVING YOUR EXCUSES BEHIND

TRAVIS HEARN

Deep River
B O O K S

CONTENTS

PREFACE

Thank you for picking up a copy of this book. I have been praying that the words and stories contained within these next ten chapters will change your life, *forever!*

Make no mistake about it, this book is not just a fun and playful title that contains "suck-it-up" *motivational* tips for your life. On the contrary, this book contains God-sized *transformational truths* that possess the power to revolutionize your life, forever! *Motivation* lasts only a moment; *transformation* lasts a lifetime.

Transformation takes place by changing the way you think. As Paul encouraged, "let God transform you into a new person by changing the way you think" (Rom. 12:2a, NLT). And when you transform the way you think, you will undoubtedly transform the way you live. Proverbs 4:23 says "Be careful how you think; your life is shaped by your thoughts" (GNT).

This book is about God's transformation process taking place within *you*. It's about you, becoming the person God has always intended for you to be. It's about you, moving from surviving in life, to thriving in life. It's about you, believing *and* achieving. It's about you, living out your wildest dreams. And most importantly, about you, living out those audacious God-sized dreams that *He* has for your life.

For thousands of years, the fact still remains true, "With God, all things are possible" (Matt. 19:26, NIV). And because of these empowering words from Jesus, I know that "I can do all things through Christ who gives me strength"—and so can you. No excuses.

INTRODUCTION

THE SIZE OF OUR BUTS

Your BUT's Too Big is about, well, obviously, your big *but*! You've got a big ol' but, and I've got a big ol' but! Think of everything you could accomplish in life, if you just didn't have that big ol' but.

The truth is, the sheer size of our buts can be paralyzing. Shoot, our buts can be so big that they even become what we're known for! And we aren't the only ones with big buts. Even beast-mode Bible bad boys had big buts! The Bible is entrenched with people who were transformed from excuse-making chumps to hall-of-faith champs. Let me give you a few examples.

In chapters three and four of Exodus, the Bible tells us about Moses' *but*. God had captivated Moses' attention by speaking to him through the burning bush. Moses was eighty years old when God supernaturally burst a bush into flames and started talking to him through the blaze. God began outlining his sovereign and exciting plan of using Moses to lead the children of Israel from out of Egyptian slavery. But even with the burning bush spectacular, Moses wasn't feeling it one bit, and so he began rattling off the excuses. Moses didn't try to hide behind just one excuse, but five! That's some serious coverage right there! What were the five excuses Moses gave to God? Let's check them out:

1. "Who am I?" (Ex. 3:11).
2. "What do I tell the people?" (3:13).
3. "What if they don't believe me or listen to me?" (4:1).

xvi Your BUT'S Too Big

4. "Lord, I'm not eloquent. I'm slow in speech and tongue" (4:10).

5. "Oh, Lord, please, send someone else to do it" (4:13).

In Judges 6, God asked Gideon to deliver the children of Israel from the hand of the Midianites, but Gideon refuted: "God, I'm too insignificant and too young. I'm of the smallest tribe, and my tribe is the poorest tribe within the poorest community!" God called Jeremiah to be a prophet to the nations; Jeremiah's excuse was, "I don't know how to speak and I'm too young."

God asked Jonah to go preach the truth, not to his own people, but to *Nineveh*, Israel's hated enemy. The Bible says:

> But Jonah ran away from the Lord and headed for Tarshish. He went down to Joppa, where he found a ship bound for that port. After paying the fare, he went aboard and sailed for Tarshish to flee from the Lord (Jonah 1:3, NIV).

Although the Bible doesn't mention what Jonah's excuses might have been, one could assume by his dramatic reaction that he had a few. I mean, he not only disobeyed the Lord—he actually paid money in order to flee in the opposite direction! And I can't say that I blame him, either. Nineveh is modern-day Mosul, Iraq. Nineveh was the capitol of Assyria and could be likened to the barbarians of ISIS. The Assyrians were bloodthirsty mass murderers who would behead their enemies and use their blood to graffiti their walls! I might have had a few excuses of my own!

And how about the excuses the disciples made when Jesus asked them to follow him in Luke 9:57–62? One potential disciple offered up the excuse, "Lord, first let me go and bury my father." Another's excuse was, "I will follow you, Lord; *but* first let me go back and say goodbye to my family."

You see, even the greatest Bible warriors were one-time babbling worriers. And it's not like they were bad excuses, either. I mean, come on, the dude's dad died, and the other one just wanted to say goodbye to his family! Seems reasonable, right? But, buts are buts—no ifs, ands or buts. And when God gives you the call, he wants it all!

This is exactly what this book is about: leaving your buts where they were meant to be—behind you! As we begin this journey together, ask yourself this question: What excuses am I making *right now* that prevent me from living out my God-sized dreams?

Listen, it's time to get that *but* out of the way once and for all and live a life of no excuses! God has a plan for your life—and nothing, I repeat nothing, should ever get in the way of that. God promises in Jeremiah 29:11: "For I know the plans I have for you," declares the LORD, "plans to prosper you and not to harm you, plans to give you hope and a future" (NIV). I love this verse! God has a plan for your life, to prosper you, to give you hope, and to give you a future!

In Philippians 4:13 God's Word also promises, "I can do all things through Christ who strengthens me" (NKJV). Did you catch that? You can do *all things* through Christ who strengthens you! That should be a shot of motivation and inspiration deep into the center of your soul! That verse singlehandedly stops every possible excuse we could ever dream up or drum up dead in its tracks! There's no excuse that should ever attempt to take the place of God's use for your life! There's nothing you can't do, because God's got you! You can do all things through Christ who strengthens you! No excuses!

As the apostle Paul boldly proclaimed in Romans 8:31, "If God is for us, who can be against us" (NIV)? And God *is* for us; so who cares who's against us? It's go-time! It's time to shake those buts once and for all!

CHAPTER ONE

BUT . . . I'M AFRAID

I've learned that you can be right smack in the middle of hell, yet feel the presence of heaven all around you.

So do not fear, for I am with you; do not be dismayed, for I am your God. I will strengthen you and help you; I will uphold you with my righteous right hand.

Isaiah 41:10, NIV

Of course, by now, you know I'm not misspelling the word *but* over and over; rather, I'm talking about our incredible ability to make excuses! I guess it's my way of having some fun with a not-so-funny pandemic that frustrates our lives. Buts. Excuses. I don't know about you, but I specialize in excuse-making; and many times, I'm simply hiding behind my own but! We all do! And one of the biggest buts we hide behind is *fear* or *worry.*

Fear is not from God. It's either created from our own human minds or from hell's helpers firing off fear flames in an effort to land them in our brains. The devil loves when we make excuses. Let's just say: The devil likes big buts and he can't *not* lie. Fear is a universal plague and is no respecter of persons. It strikes the young and the old, the rich and the poor. When fear strikes, it debilitates even the most driven of individuals and demotivates the most motivated. Fear is a powerful, deadly, and highly contagious disease. You can contract it from others and you can contaminate others. Fear

1

can spread through friendships, families and organizations faster than a deadly cancer can disseminate through the human body.

The Merriam-Webster's Dictionary defines *fear* as: to expect or *worry* about something bad or unpleasant, or to be afraid and *worried*. Scary, right? We actually *expect* the bad and unpleasant. And we tend to expect and imagine the worst. I don't know why we do this, but we do. It's like when you receive a letter from the IRS and you go into sheer panic! I've been there—haven't you? But perhaps, it's simply a statement. We seem to expect the worst. We *worry* about the bad and unpleasant.

Interestingly enough, the word *worry* comes from an Old English word that means to *strangle* or *choke*. The ancestor of our word, Old English *wyrgan,* meant "to strangle." Its Middle English descendant, *worien,* kept this sense and developed the new sense "to grasp by the throat with the teeth and lacerate" or "to kill or injure by biting and shaking." This is the way wolves or dogs might attack sheep, for example. In the sixteenth century *worry* began to be used in the sense of "harass, as by rough treatment or attack," or "to assault verbally"; and in the seventeenth century the word took on the sense of "bother, distress, or persecute." It was a small step from this sense to the main modern senses "to cause to feel anxious or distressed" and "to feel troubled or uneasy," first recorded in the nineteenth century.

What a gruesomely chilling and frightening visual! Worry grasps you by the throat, and attempts to choke, strangle, bite, lacerate, and shake the peace and joy right out of your life. Fear puts its tight grip around your mind as it constricts like a snake and shakes your soul vigorously with the full intent of ending in death and destruction. Death to peace and joy, death to clarity of mind, death to a rested soul and comfort, and even death to your physical body.

Chances are good that, right now, you're worrying about something—potentially about everything. Maybe you're worried about your relationship, your job or finances; maybe you're worried about your health, or a loved one. Maybe you're worried about worrying!

Everyone lives with worries. Everyone lives with fears. But not everyone has to be debilitated or die because of them. Whatever it is that you're worried about or afraid of today; it's important that you understand that the devil would love nothing more than to use fear to choke and strangle the comfort and sanity right out of your mind. There are millions of Christians going to heaven today, and the only possible victory for the devil is to try to make you live through hell while you're on earth. He'll take it where he can get it. The devil doesn't need to scare you to death if he can scare you into not living. God cautions us to pay attention and to be alert. "Be alert and of sober mind. Your enemy the devil prowls around like a roaring lion looking for someone to devour" (1 Peter 5:8, NIV).

Fear Makes You Freak

I read a funny joke about two blondes. (My mom and sisters are blondes, so I dedicate this one to you guys!) There were two blondes traveling in an airplane from LA to New York. About an hour into the flight, the pilot announced that they had lost an engine, but not to worry, there are three left! However, instead of five hours it would take seven hours to get to New York. A little later, he announced that a second engine failed, but, not to worry, as they still had two left. Now it would take ten hours to get to New York. Somewhat later, the pilot again came on the intercom and announced that a third engine had died. No worries, he announced, because the plane could fly on a single engine. However, it would now take eighteen hours to get to New York. At this point, the one blonde turned to the other and said, "Oh my goodness, I'm worried sick. I hope we don't lose that last engine, or we'll be up here forever!" (Okay, "funny" was probably a stretch.)

Look, I don't know about you, but I've spent way too much of my life worrying! I've worried about life-bombs that never blew up. I've worried about what other people might think, what other people have said, what I've said, job interviews, deadlines, budgets, bills and expenses, rising gas prices, war, and even the end of the world! (Yes, I've worried about the end of the world—once.) I don't consider myself a compulsive worrier, although I certainly exercise my fair share of worrying. I share this next story with you reluctantly, for the fear that you might think substantially less of me—and that worries me.

Let's just say that I was thoroughly prepared for Y2K! In 1999, I listened to a well-respected pastor preach about the possibility of the world's computer systems shutting down at the strike of the year 2000. He didn't say that the computer systems were absolutely undeniably going to shut down, he just mentioned that this was a theory floating around. However, my ears heard, "The freakin' sky is falling!" Maybe it was because this wasn't just *any* pastor; he was a former big shot from Microsoft, which meant to me, this idea might have some weight to it! And the more I listened, the more that strangling, choking grasp wrapped itself around my mind and put the squeeze on. Panic set in and started growing like a wild weed on steroids, and fear made me freak! I thought to myself, "The world's coming to an end! Computers are going to shut down globally! This means electricity will shut down. The water systems won't function. Grocery stores will be raided, looted, and depleted! Famine's about to strike! My friendly neighbors are going to turn into *war enemies!*" Marshal law's gonna kick in! Well then, it's go-time! Let's do this! It's on like Donkey Kong eatin' a ding dong! Bring. It. On.

And so the preparation began! And as I watched that ball drop to catapult us into the year 2000, I was ready. In fact, I had more tuna than Costco! I had more weapons and ammunition than the Russians (okay, well not quite that expansive!). And if my unprepared friendly neighbor would have approached my house and tried to snake my tuna—I was prepared to snipe that joker from a makeshift bunker on the top of my house! (I'm joking, of course; I would have come down to the ground, led him to the Lord first, and *then* shot him at point blank!) It seems like just yesterday, but as those final seconds ticked off that clock, there I was—relieved, yet feeling like a complete idiot. I remember thinking, "Wow, somebody just made a boatload of money by targeting the fears of man."

Yep, I've wasted so much of my time worrying about worries that never happened! I've worried about contagious infections, identity theft, first impressions, political correctness, all kinds of stuff. But guess what? I'm still here today, alive and well. My bills are paid, my family is healthy, and I also have plenty of food— probably because I'm still eating tuna! I've learned that worrying doesn't work, and that today's the tomorrow you worried about yesterday.

Worry Doesn't Work

Maybe the most asinine issue about worrying is that—worry doesn't work! It's proven to be a highly ineffective strategy for problem-solving, if we can even label it a strategy. As Mark Twain said, "My life has been filled with calamities, some of which actually happened." Researchers at the University of Cincinnati found that eighty-five percent of what we worry about *never happens*. I realize that for those of you who are compulsive worriers, I just freaked the mess right out of you right now and you're thinking, "Oh my word! There's still a fifteen percent chance this could happen?" If this is you, you can relax because some studies show that up to ninety percent of what we worry about never actually happens— and that we can find a solution for the other ten percent.

Worry doesn't work. Jesus tried to drive this point home for us in Matthew 6:25–34 (NIV) when he said:

> Therefore I tell you, do not worry about your life, what you will eat or drink; or about your body, what you will wear. Is not life more than food, and the body more than clothes? Look at the birds of the air; they do not sow or

reap or store away in barns, and yet your heavenly Father
feeds them. Are you not much more valuable than they?
Can any one of you by worrying add a single hour to your
life?

And why do you worry about clothes? See how the
flowers of the field grow. They do not labor or spin. Yet
I tell you that not even Solomon in all his splendor was
dressed like one of these. If that is how God clothes the
grass of the field, which is here today and tomorrow is
thrown into the fire, will he not much more clothe you—
you of little faith? So do not worry, saying, "What shall
we eat?" or "What shall we drink?" or "What shall we
wear?" For the pagans run after all these things, and your
heavenly Father knows that you need them. But seek first
his kingdom and his righteousness, and all these things
will be given to you as well. Therefore do not worry
about tomorrow, for tomorrow will worry about itself.
Each day has enough trouble of its own.

Worry Makes It Worse

Not only does worry not work—worry makes the worry worse!
Worry is toxic. Trying to extinguish your problems by worrying is
like trying to extinguish a raging fire by drenching it in gasoline.
Worrying is like staring at your fear through a magnifying glass
and never blinking. Worry amplifies, not satisfies. Worry beats
you down mentally, emotionally, and physically to where you feel
like you've gone through a war. Because you have. Worry makes
things worse.

My grandmother is in her 80s and I am extremely close to her.
But grandma hasn't driven a car since she was in her 30s. Why?
Because she was struck hard by another car and it scared her—
not to death, but to stop driving. The fear and worry of getting in
another car wreck has literally prevented her from ever driving a car

ever again. And I don't blame her. For the last fifty years, Grandpa has done all the driving. Worry amplifies, not satisfies.

I heard about a CEO who worried all the time. He was talking to his colleague and he said, "Guess what!? I've fixed my worries and I don't worry anymore."

His buddy said, "Oh yeah? How'd you do that?"

The CEO replied, "I hired a professional worrier. I write down all my worries, and he worries for me."

"Wow, what a great idea! How much does that cost?"

"$250,000 a year."

His buddy said, "250 grand?! And how on earth are you gonna pay for that?"

The CEO said, "I have no idea—that's for him to worry about now!"

I know, I know, the cheese is thick up in here! But paying someone else to worry for you wouldn't work. Then again, neither would worrying.

The Valley's Not the Finale

> *"Even though I walk through the valley of the shadow of death...."*

Those words of David are so famous and full of hope that three thousand years after they were written, they're still being used today by people all over the world in funeral services, books, sermons, and songs. In fact, this verse is found in songs by hardcore rap artists like Tupac and The Notorious B.I.G., as well as well-known worship leaders like Jeremy Camp and Matt Redman. If you begin typing "psalm" into any search-engine box, Psalm 23 is the first one to pop up.

Without a doubt, the most famous psalm has also proven to be one of the most quoted passages not only in the book of Psalms, but in the entire Bible. Why? Because these powerful scriptures infuse peace, hope, and courage deep into the soul of every fearful and worried set of eyes that reads them. Psalm 23 is God's written proof to us that he doesn't want us to worry.

> Even though I walk through the valley of the shadow of death, I will fear no evil, for you are with me" (Psalm 23:4, ESV).

Ah, the valley. David uses a brilliant metaphor for the dark and scary times of our lives. It's the perfect imagery to describe the worries, fears, and anxieties of life. The valley. But for David, it wasn't just metaphorical imagery; it was also geographical reality. In Israel, there is an actual Valley of the Shadow of Death. Picture the Grand Canyon, in Arizona, only smaller. The Valley of the Shadow of Death is an extremely narrow, winding, dark path with enormous cliffs on both sides. In fact, only at high noon, when the sun beats directly overhead, does sunlight hit the bottom of the canyon. Shepherds would lead their sheep through this valley as thieves and bandits would hide along the top of the hill in caves and crevices waiting to attack and steal their sheep. This wasn't just an artistic writer's analogy; it was a geographical location that David was well aware of. Who knows, maybe David led his sheep through this valley as a boy and experienced its fear firsthand.

The valley is a fitting and relatable illustration loaded with timeless principles for the dark and scary times we all go through in life. We *all* go through the valleys of life. Nobody is exempt. Even Jesus said it rains on both the just and the unjust (Matt. 5:45). Valleys are where the thief of our soul hides, lurking and waiting for our arrival with the sole objective to steal, kill, and destroy us.

Look at it again: "Even though I walk through the valley of the shadow of death, I will fear no evil, for you are with me." This verse is charged full of hope! Within this message of faith from King David lie three extremely powerful *highlights of hope* I'd like to draw to your attention.

The first highlight of hope is that the *valley is not the finale*. David used the phrase "walk *through* the valley" and not "*to* the valley." The difference between the word *through* and *to* is the difference between hope and hopelessness. Whatever you're going *through* today, I'm here to tell you that you're going *through* it. The other side awaits you. I pray that truth resonates deep in your soul! Fear is not final. Worry is not final. Your situation is not final. There is always hope to head toward. I promise, you will get through this!

I love the fact that David also used the word "walk." He didn't say, "Even though I run as fast as I can through the valley,", "Even though I sprint desperately through the valley," or "Even though I panic and turn around and run right back out of the valley." He said, "even though I *walk* through the valley." It's almost as if David depicts a God-sized confidence welling up within us as we walk with complete swagger and unshaken *faith* directly into the face of fear.

Keep walking. You'll get there! You're going *through*, you're not going *to*. The valley is not the finale.

It's Just a Shadow

The second highlight of hope is that *it's just a shadow*. Whew! David said, "Even though I walk through the valley of the *shadow* of death." He didn't say, "The valley of death." Thank God!

It may feel like death, it may look like death, and it might even smell like death, but it's not death—it's just a shadow. And there are three quick truths I'd like to bring to light (no pun intended) about shadows:

Shadows are bigger than reality. I remember when my daughter Jazzlyn was two years old and was laying down for bedtime. She began screaming in complete fear! I ran as fast as my body could take me to her room. Her eyes were the size of the moon. She was pointing at the wall and there he was: a big, dark, scary monster slithering up her wall! Oh, he was creepy! Only it wasn't a *he*—it was a *she!* Indeed, her favorite baby dolly was sitting on the ground casting the shadow of a giant scary monster! Shadows are *always* bigger than reality.

Shadows can't hurt you. The church I pastor in Arizona, Impact Church, is located in the Scottsdale Airpark. Literally, outside my office window, jets take off and land all throughout the day. Powerful jets. Noisy jets. Jets that rattle and shake the entire building. And jet shadows fly over top of me and our church building every single day. And you know what? They might shake me, but they don't break me. Shadows have never hurt me. Not once have I ever been injured by a shadow. And neither have you.

Where there is a shadow—there is always a light. Here's an idea that will set you free: Stop looking at the shadows! Why is it that when there's something scary, tragic, or gruesome in life, we can't keep our eyes off it? It's like a bad car wreck. People slow down and congest the entire freeway so they can take a little look-see at how bad the damage is.

Listen: Anywhere there's a shadow, there's always a light. Look for the light! Turn your eyes and body away from the shadow and away from your fears, and face the light so that the shadow will fall directly behind you. Remember these calming and soothing words of Jesus in John 8:12 (NIV), "I am the light of the world. Whoever follows me will never walk in darkness, but will have the light of life."

God Is with You

The third and most exciting highlight of hope is *God is with you!* That's the game changer. That should be music to your ears. That should give you all the confidence in the world to walk straight into the face of hell because God is with you. God's got you!

All three of my kids will attempt far more daring and frightening challenges with daddy by their side than they would ever attempt *without* daddy by their side. Don't get me wrong, they're pretty brave little soldiers, but with Daddy by their side they become Rambos.

Last summer, we were teaching my youngest daughter Jazzlyn to swim. I asked her to jump off the side of the pool and into the water. She said, "I don't want to, Daddy, I'm scared!"

I said, "You want Daddy to go with you and hold your hand and jump in with you?"

"Yes."

I stuck out my hand. She put her tiny little hand into the palm of mine and I counted, "1, 2, 3, jump!"

Splash! She jumped in with me. After that, she must have jumped fifty times on her own, without me.

That is exactly the confidence that we have with God. God's got you. He is with you! Remember Psalm 16:8 (NIV), "I keep my eyes always on the LORD. With him at my right hand, I will not be shaken."

When you fully understand that God is with you, it changes the way you do life. It changes the way you think; it changes the way you walk; it changes the way you walk through valleys. I've learned that you can be right smack in the middle of hell, yet feel the presence of heaven all around you. God's peace will always protect you from the beast.

I'm fascinated by what the apostle Paul penned while he was in prison in Rome, "And the peace of God, which transcends all understanding, will guard your hearts and your minds in Christ Jesus" (Philippians 4:6–7, NIV). And let's not forget everything else that Paul had been through. In his own words, he had:

> … been in prison more frequently, been flogged more severely, and been exposed to death again and again. Five times I received from the Jews the forty lashes minus one. Three times I was beaten with rods, once I was pelted with stones, three times I was shipwrecked,

I spent a night and a day in the open sea, I have been constantly on the move. I have been in danger from rivers,
in danger from bandits, in danger from my fellow Jews,
in danger from Gentiles; in danger in the city, in danger
in the country, in danger at sea; and in danger from false
believers. I have labored and toiled and have often gone
without sleep; I have known hunger and thirst and have
often gone without food; I have been cold and naked. (2
Corinthians 11:23–27, NIV)

And yet he said, "And the peace of God, which transcends
all understanding, will guard your hearts and your minds in Christ
Jesus." Wow! How could Paul have possibly possessed so much
strength? In some ways, that passage makes me feel like I have
featherweight faith! In other ways, however, it gives me a glimpse of
hope and promise to think that "I can do all things through Christ
who strengthens me."

How did Paul possess such strength and peace while he was
in prison? Paul actually didn't possess such strength. God did, and
Paul figured out how to tap into it. That same God is my strength
and your strength. Paul had awesome perspective when he said,
"That is why, for Christ's sake, I delight in weaknesses, in insults, in
hardships, in persecutions, in difficulties. For when I am weak, then
I am strong" (2 Corinthians 12:10, NIV).

Rally in the Valley

It's time to put your rally caps on, because these three highlights of
hope set us up for a rally in the valley! So huddle up, put your hands
in the middle, let's get a break, and get our Jesus on! Lift up your
head, turn your face to the sky, and put that smile back on your face!
The valley's not the finale, it's just a shadow, and God is with you!

Deuteronomy 31:8 promises that God will never leave you and
never forsake you. That's two "never"s in one verse! I take that to
mean, never! Proverbs 18:24 assures us, "God is a friend who sticks

closer than a brother" (AKJV). God's got you! Yes, God's—got—
you. The same God who created the universe. The same God who
flung and hung the stars into the middle of the sky. The same God
who spun the sun into space, a burning ball of plasma that's always
burning, yet never burns up. Do you know how big the sun is? You
could fit 109 earths across the face of the sun. And do you know
how big God is? He's the God of the impossible and the God of
the supernatural. He's the God who raises the dead and he's the
God who rose from the dead. That's how big he is! And *that* God—
he's got you!

Listen, I don't know what you're going through, but your situation didn't take God by surprise. It might have taken you by
surprise, but whatever you're worrying about right now, it didn't
catch God off guard. This always brings me peace of mind and it
should do the same for you. God knows everything about everything. He's omniscient, and yet he loves you and cares for you
and every worry in your life. Your jacked-up situation didn't catch
God off guard. It's not like God's sitting up in heaven playing
golf or surfing the eternal web and then one day says, "Wait, what
just happened? Moses! Did you guys just hear the news? She's in
the middle of a crisis! He just lost everything!" No: God knows
what's going to happen before *happen* ever happens. He's got eternal vision. He can see down the road and he's got perfect perspective. Look what David said about this:

> LORD, you have examined me and know all about me.
> You know when I sit down and when I get up. You know
> my thoughts before I think them. You know where I go
> and where I lie down. You know everything I do. LORD,
> even before I say a word, you already know it. You are all
> around me—in front and in back. . . . Your knowledge is
> amazing to me; it is more than I can understand. Where
> can I go to get away from your Spirit? Where can I run
> from you? If I go up to the heavens, you are there. If

I lie down in the grave, you are there. (Psalm 139:1–8, NCV)

See? God's got you! As Martin Luther King said, "I don't know what the future holds, but I do know who holds the future." In life, you can never walk down a road where God isn't there. He's the real road king.

In my house, we have a picture that hangs in the hallway as we leave the house. It reads: "The will of God will never take you where the grace of God will not protect you." I look at that picture all the time. Sometimes it just hangs there and whispers to me. Other times it screams at me. There are days when I really need to read that again. There are days when it's a great reminder for me. The will of God will never take you where the grace of God will not protect you. You can never go down a road where God isn't with you. So have courage, don't be afraid. God told Joshua, "I command you—be strong and courageous! Do not be afraid or discouraged. For the LORD your God is with you wherever you go" (Joshua 1:9, NLT). God's got you!

Get Your Mind off Yourself

I get it; we're selfish. I basically think about *me* all the time. I think about *my* health, *my* safety, *my* family, *my* finances, *my* church, my-oh-my! It's disgusting. I pretty much do the exact opposite of what Philippians 2:3 (NIV) instructs me to do, "Do nothing out of selfish ambition or vain conceit. Rather, in humility value others above yourselves." Yep, I do the opposite. If we're honest, most of us do. Maybe that's why I worry so much. Maybe that's why I'm afraid so often. I think about *me* the greater majority of the time.

But I have learned something about myself: What brings me the greatest joy in my life and the greatest peace in my life is when I'm not thinking about myself, and instead thinking about others. No wonder Jesus mentioned in Matthew 22:39, "Love your neighbor as yourself." Come on, admit it. That's tough. We love ourselves. Some people love themselves so much that nobody else likes them. But if you want to minimize your worries and fears, you've got to get your mind off yourself and put it on others.

Four Keys to Leaving the "BUT . . . I'm Afraid" Excuse behind You

So here's to the new and healthier you; to getting rid of that *but* once and for all! Here's to making sure your fears and worries aren't excuses that keep you from living out those God-sized dreams for your life, and from living a life full of peace, joy, and happiness. I encourage you to apply these four *but*-kickin' principles to your life, and watch that *but* get smaller right before your very eyes.

#1—Instead Of *Worry*, Read God's *Word*

It's amazing how the person whose Bible is falling apart, usually isn't. There's nothing in the world more refreshing and relaxing than God's Word. It's alive and active and pervaded with God's protection, direction, inspection, and correction. When you're going through the valley, remember the words of Psalm 119:105 (NIV), "Your word is a lamp for my feet, a light on my path."

The Bible says in Proverbs 12:25 (NIV), "An anxious heart weighs a man down, but a kind word cheers him up." Let me tell you something: There is no kinder word than *God's Word*. Whether you're having moments or a lifestyle of fear or worry, I highly recommend diving into your Bible and allowing God's Word to work out the worry in your life. Read God's Word daily. Study it, meditate on it, and memorize it. This is how Joshua faced *his* fears. In Joshua 1:8 (NIV) he said, "Keep this Book of the Law always on your lips; meditate on it day and night, so that you may be careful to do everything written in it."

The Word of God is so important for our lives that Moses said, "Place these words on your hearts. Get them deep inside you. Tie them on your hands and foreheads as a reminder. Teach them to your children. Talk about them wherever you are, sitting at home or walking in the street; talk about them from the time you get up in the morning until you fall into bed at night" (Deut. 18–19, MES).

So first things first. Instead of worry, read God's Word.

#2—Instead of Panic, Give God Praise

If there's ever a moment in my life when I'm not worried or afraid, it's when I'm sitting in the presence of God, singing praises, focusing my mind and attention on him, and not me or my circumstances. You lose your fear when Jesus is near. It's during praise where I tell God how absolutely impressive he is, how much I love him, and how thankful I am for him. It seems to minimize everything I'm going through.

I take some time out of my day to glorify God, to simply adore Jesus, and to give him thanks for all He's done, all he's doing and all he's going to do, *no matter the outcome*. It's a way for me to take a deep breath and say, "God, my life is in your hands and I trust you with it." I always find strength and rest in his presence and in giving him praise. Jesus said: "Come to me, all you who are weary and burdened, and I will give you rest. Take my yoke upon you and learn from me, for I am gentle and humble in heart, and you will find rest for your souls. For my yoke is easy and my burden is light" (Matthew 11:28–30, NIV).

One of my all-time favorite verses that is a must-memorize is found in Isaiah 40:31 (KJV): "But they that wait upon the Lord shall renew their strength; they shall mount up with wings as eagles; they shall run, and not be weary; and they shall walk, and not faint."

So instead of worry, read God's Word; and instead of panic, give God praise!

#3—Instead of Terror, Take It to the Lord in Prayer

The choice is yours. You can freak out or you can speak out! I say, "Pray!" The fact of the matter is: Prayer works. But isn't it amazing how we all know prayer works, yet we all have plenty of room left to increase our prayer lives.

Listen: Prayer doesn't work when your prayer lives are broken. Prayer doesn't work if you don't pray.

There's a story of a ship that was sinking in the middle of a storm, and the captain called out to the crew and said, "Does anyone here know how to pray?" One man stepped forward and said, "Yes sir, I know how to pray." The captain said, "Wonderful, you pray while the rest of us put on life jackets—we're one short!" Ha!

We all know prayer works, so let's get our praise on and let's get our pray on! When you're in a moment of terror, take it to God in prayer. "Don't worry about anything; instead, pray about everything. Tell God what you need, and thank him for all he has done. Then you will experience God's peace" (Phil. 4:6–7, NLT).

Instead of worry, read God's Word; instead of panic, give God praise; and instead of prayer, take it to the Lord in prayer. Finally:

#4—Instead of Fear, Step out in Faith

This goes hand-in-hand with point number 1 because the Bible says, "So then faith comes by hearing, and hearing by the word of God" (Rom. 10:17, NKJV). If you want more faith and less fear, read God's Word, study God's Word, and memorize God's Word. Faith is like a muscle—the more you use it, the stronger it becomes. And that's exactly the goal: smaller fear, bigger faith. No excuses! Smaller buts and bigger guts!

Remember the turtle; he only makes progress when he sticks his neck out! Faith and fear cannot coexist with one another. Choose faith. Choose love. "God is love. There is no fear in love. But perfect love casts out all fear" (1 John 4:8, 18, ESV).

There. Feeling a bit better? I've prayed so. Your *but* is slimmer and trimmer already.

CHAPTER TWO

BUT . . . I'M HURTING

It's by the thorn, dependency is born.

I was given a thorn in my flesh, a messenger of Satan, to torment me. Three times I pleaded with the Lord to take it away from me. But he said to me, "My grace is sufficient for you, for my power is made perfect in weakness." Therefore I will boast all the more gladly about my weaknesses, so that Christ's power may rest on me.

2 Corinthians 12:7–9, NIV

There's never a pain in vain. *But,* if there ever was a good enough reason to have a big but, it'd certainly be pain. I mean, really, how can we possibly work on our buts if we are in so much physical pain we can't even function, or because we're in so much emotional pain we can't even think straight?

But the bottom line is that there *is* no good reason for excuses. Not one. After all, it was through pain and a torturous crucifixion that Jesus set the world free. Many times, the very thing that you think is destroying you is simply God's process of anointing you. Anointing oil is produced from the crushing of an olive, and when the olive is crushed, the oil begins to flow.

Three Types of Major Pains

C. S. Lewis nailed it when he said, "God whispers to us in our pleasure but He shouts to us in our pain." Pain is God's megaphone. In fact, in the words of Rick Warren, "Sometimes, the only way God can get you to look up, is to lay you flat on your back." Let's be honest, hurts . . . hurt. And when I'm hurting, God's got my attention. I'm convinced that there's never a time in your life that you are closer to God than when you're in pain. *There's never a time in life when you're closer to Christ than when you are in the middle of a crisis.*

I'm also convinced that our prayer lives are never as strong as when we are in pain. Personally, every time I'm in pain, I ask God to take it away. Every time. He's probably thinking, "Travis, why would I take your pain away? I never have this much attention from you and spend so much time with you any other time." There's always a purpose behind the pain. The hurts and pains we suffer are much deeper than just being about *us* and the discomfort that we're going through.

It's important to understand the three major types of pain every human being experiences: physical, emotional, and spiritual. Unfortunately, if you're alive and have a heartbeat, you'll live through each of these. I don't know what type of pain and hurt you're going through today, but I'd like to reiterate two things: There's never a pain in vain; and God wants you to use your hurts to help others. When you've been hurt deeply by others, you can hurt deeply for others.

In fact, it's the very life Jesus lived. Even *he* wasn't exempt. The Bible says, "he was pierced for our transgressions, he was crushed for our iniquities; the punishment that brought us peace was on him, and by his wounds we are healed" (Isaiah 53:5, NIV). Jesus experienced the deepest level of pain for all of humanity as he was crucified for the sins of the world.

BUT I'm Physically Hurting

I'm in pain. Severe pain. Excruciating pain. Daily, chronic pain. In my previous book, *Game Changer*, I mentioned that I have a lingering neck condition that I've been managing since I was twenty-one years old. I know many people undoubtedly suffer far more severe pain than I do, and I always try to keep that in perspective, but it's the most excruciating pain I've ever felt in my life. It feels like a stabbing, sharp fork, or maybe more like snake fangs that have penetrated into the inner core of my spine—and they never go away. Doctors have diagnosed me with bulging disks, degenerative disks, arthritis, and other medical-science jargon that I don't know how to spell or pronounce. It affects everything in my daily life, and boy, do I mean everything. It not only affects *my* life, but it affects my wife's life, my kids' lives, and the lives of those closest to me. If you are somebody who suffers from a medical problem or chronic pain, my heart goes out to you. *My* pain has opened my eyes to the world of people in pain.

I have been to chiropractors, MDs, DOs, and everything in between. Nothing has fixed the problem. I have frequent procedures performed called epidural injections, and I've even had a procedure done called Radiofrequency Ablation (RFA), where the doctor burns the nerves in half in the affected c-spine area by the use of needles and radio frequency activity. Unfortunately, that didn't seem to help either. I've asked God to heal me, at least several thousand times, but here I am with the same excruciating pain. And the fact is, I'll keep praying, keep believing, keep trying trustworthy procedures, but I just might die with this pain.

My neck condition is not only a pain in my butt, but also in my *but*. When I think of my pain, I'm reminded over and again of the words of the apostle Paul, "I was given a thorn in my flesh, a messenger of Satan, to torment me. Three times I pleaded with the Lord to take it away from me. But he said to me, 'My grace is sufficient for you, for my power is made perfect in weakness'" (2 Cor. 12:7–9, NIV). And that's exactly how I feel; my agonizing neck pain is a messenger straight from the pit of hell sent to torment *me*. It's ironic because the three things that intensify my pain the most are sleep, writing sermons or books, and preaching. Isn't that just like the devil? The devil literally is a pain in my neck. The very thing that God has called me to do leaves me feeling as if snake venom has been shot into my neck! It's the thorn in my flesh.

But there's hope! There's always hope. I find myself clinging to those powerful words of hope in that same scripture every single day of my life, "My grace is sufficient for you." And God's grace *is* sufficient. It's always been and will always be. The other promise in this scripture that I cling to is, "My power is made perfect in my weakness"—God's power, that is, made perfect in *my* weakness. The fact is, with every night of sleep I get, every sermon or article I write, and every chapter of a book I complete, God's power was just made perfect in my weakness. I've learned that *it's by the thorn, dependency is born.* The thorn reminds me that I am completely and wholeheartedly dependent on God and his grace. The thorn also reminds me that each day I have the privilege of tapping into God's unmerited grace because of my savior who died with a head full of thorns.

I understand when people talk about hurts and pains. And I have a much greater compassion now for people who suffer with pain. There have been many times when someone who didn't even know about my pain or condition, reached out to me with tear-filled eyes and asked me to pray for their chronic neck or back condition. It is in these moments that I realized that there's never a pain in vain and that God wants me to use my hurts to help others. People who have been hurt deeply *by* others can hurt deeply *with* others. As Paul said, "God comforts us in all our troubles so that we can comfort others. When others are troubled, we will be able to give them the same comfort God has given us. So, when we are weighed down with troubles, it is for your benefit . . . so that we can be an encouragement to you." (2 Cor. 1:4, 6, NLT). Through the eyes and lenses of my personal hurts and pains, I've been able to pray with deep conviction, passion, and compassion, and have even witnessed God remove Satan's thorny, tormenting messenger from other people's flesh. You know what else? It's because of my pain that I've also had the privilege of sharing the love of God with doctors, nurses, chiropractors, and physical therapists.

Whatever physical hurts you might have today, I've prayed for you. I prayed in advance of you even picking up this book, that every person who is in physical pain who reads these words would receive complete supernatural healing, in Jesus' name.

I also want to encourage you to hang in there and keep on keepin' on. Keep praying and pressing in. Never give up! Never toss in the towel! Fight the good fight (2 Tim. 4:7), and finish the race. Turn your physical pain into a platform for God's name. God's grace is sufficient for you, and his power is made perfect in your weakness.

BUT I'm Emotionally Hurting

It's hard to physically move when you're emotionally paralyzed, and it's hard to physically breathe when you're emotionally suffocating. That's how Satan would love for you to stay: a suffocated paralytic who is going to heaven but lives hell on earth. What a slick and clever tactic the enemy would love to use on *you* to keep you locked down with excuses. And that's precisely why this won't be you! God is bigger than our emotional pain. And "greater is he that is in you, than he that is in the world" (1 John 4:4, KJV).

The reality is that we are emotional beings, and that emotional pain hurts just as bad as physical pain, if not more. Emotional hurts can have long-lasting and devastating effects (although with Jesus in the mix, they aren't supposed to). Emotional hurts and pains reside within the complex layers of our emotional realm. They can be caused by human experiences like divorce or breakups, the death of a loved one, someone being diagnosed with a grave illness, abuse, being humiliated or degraded, or even the emotional pains and hurts associated with failure.

Unfortunately, your emotions will cause hurt throughout your life; and no doubt, it hurts! But the real test is not the pain. Rather, it's in how you respond to pain.

Jesus was emotionally hurt, too. That's right, God has emotions too! In fact, Jesus went through all sorts of emotions during his time on earth—compassion, sympathy, affection, gladness, love, joy, peace, anger, anguish, grief, sadness, trouble, and weariness, to name just some of them. God is emotional, and the emotions he experienced on earth weren't always pleasant ones. For example, think about what it must have been like for Jesus when the very world he created didn't even recognize or receive him: "The true light that gives light to everyone was coming into the world. He was in the world, and though the world was made through him, the world did not recognize him. He came to that which was his own, but his own did not receive him" (John 1:9–11, NIV). Or when his own people drove him out of his hometown (Luke 4:29). Or when many of His disciples turned their backs on him and no longer followed him (John 6:66). Not only that, but one of Jesus' very best friends within his inner circle, Peter, denied even knowing him three times (Luke 22:57).

And yet, the deepest emotional pain Jesus felt and suffered was undoubtedly during the time when he also suffered his deepest physical pain, at his crucifixion. "'He himself bore our sins'" in his body on the cross, so that we might die to sins and live for righteousness; 'by his wounds you have been healed'" (1 Peter 2:24, NIV). Isn't it crazy to think that in order for Jesus to give us the life we never deserved, we had to give him the death *he* never deserved? Wow.

Imagine the shattering emotions Jesus must have felt as he was sold out and betrayed by one of his twelve disciples, Judas. Imagine the emotions of Jesus when he was illegally arrested, indicted, and tried. Imagine the emotions of Jesus when he was murdered by capital punishment for a crime he didn't commit by the very people he created. Imagine the distress he went through when the Roman soldiers were hammering the nails into his hands and feet over and over, or the emotional devastation he suffered when he was whipped, insulted, mocked and publicly humiliated. Jesus may have been thinking, "I remember fearfully and wonderfully creating each one of you inside your mother's womb" (see Psalm 139:14).

No doubt, Jesus suffered far more physical and emotional pain than any other human in the history of the world. He experienced betrayal, hatred, mockery, rejection, humiliation . . . and the list keeps going. But again, the real test is not experiencing or living through pain; rather, it's how we respond to pain. As our bloodied and beaten Savior hung on the cross with eyes of ridicule and derision staring him down, he possessed the love, compassion, and strength to utter these words, "Father, forgive them, for they do not know what they are doing." And that verse, Luke 23:34, is the two-part sermon Jesus left us with in how we respond when somebody hurts us.

Point #1: When somebody hurts us, we should take it to God and *pray* about it. Jesus' first word he uttered was, "Father." He didn't curse the cursing crowds from the cross. He didn't look to the thieves hanging on each side of him and start bad-mouthing everybody. He said, "Father." This is first point and the starting point. Pray about your emotional hurts and pains. *If you're gonna heal, you've gotta kneel.* Prayer is the way you repair.

When you commit your emotional hurts and pains to God, remember the reassuring words offered in Psalm 34:18 (NIV), "The LORD is near to the brokenhearted and saves the crushed in spirit." If you are broken or crushed today, know that God is near. Never allow even the deepest of emotional hurts to be a *but* in your life that keeps you from living out the God-sized dream for your life.

Point #2: The second point from Jesus' sermon is to *forgive*. Jesus said, "Forgive them." I realize this is easier said than done, but if someone has hurt you, forgiveness is the key to set you free. If you don't forgive, you won't truly live; you'll become bitter and resentful. And I've got news for you: Becoming bitter and resentful only hurts you, not the other person. S.I. McMillan wrote a book called *None of These Diseases* that talks about the effect of resentment on our bodies, and makes this point: It's not what you eat, it's what's eating you. Job said, "To worry yourself to death with resentment would be a foolish, senseless thing to do" (Job 5:2, GNT). Paul said, "Be ready to forgive. Never hold grudges. Remember the Lord forgave you so you must forgive others" (Col. 3:13, LB).

First Corinthians 13, "the love chapter" in the Bible, talks about forgiveness. Paul said this about love, "It does not dishonor others, it is not self-seeking, it is not easily angered, it keeps no record of wrongs" (1 Cor. 13:5, NIV). Years ago, I was talking to a gentleman who had been married to his wife for sixty years. That's unheard of these days. I asked him, "So tell me, what the key to staying married for sixty years?"

I was expecting some deep philosophical answer as he looked at me with a smile and said, "Short-term memory." Again, love keeps no record of wrongs.

Jesus forgave. Jesus forgives. I have a feeling there's going to be countless mind-boggling stories of God's forgiveness that we're going to hear when we get to heaven. Wouldn't it be incredible to be in heaven face-to-face with the Roman soldier who drove those nails through the hands and feet of Jesus? Listening to him tell the story of how he mistakenly murdered the Son of God and how Christ forgave him with unconditional love? It wouldn't surprise me to see him there. Can you imagine, one day in heaven, seeing the guy who smashed the crown of thorns onto the head of Jesus in mockery of his royalty and His claim as king of the Jews? I can. I can also envision seeing him in heaven one day kneeling at the feet of Jesus with his arms held high singing, "King of kings, Lord of Lords, I worship You." Because that is exactly the God we serve! A God of unmerited grace. A God of forgiveness. A God of healing. A God full of unconditional love. And that's how we must be, too.

BUT . . . I'm in Terminal Pain

I have personally shared in the sorrows and joys (yes, joys!) of many friends and family members who were terminally ill—some whom God healed and extended their life on earth, others whom God eternally healed as He couldn't stand to live another day without them in his physical presence. As a pastor, I've prayed with many individuals in the hospital or in hospice who were terminally ill. Obviously, terminal illness is a mixture of pain, both physical and emotional, that goes beyond devastation. When someone is diagnosed with terminal illness, the pain and fear can be indescribable. Shock and disbelief take over as those who are ill, and their families, enter crisis mode and walk through enormous amounts of grief and pain.

As shattering as terminal illness is—and it is—I'd like to make an audacious attempt in reorienting your thinking. The truth is, at some point we will all pass from this earthly life into our eternal life. Some of us go sooner than later; others of us will go later than sooner. But the good news is that the death of a loved one is never the end of their life. Sure, it's the end of their life on earth, but it's the beginning of their life for eternity. It's never a goodbye; rather, it's simply a "see ya' later," and the beginning of a pain-free eternal life. The exciting and encouraging reality is that we will spend *far* more time on the other side of our life in heaven with our loved ones than we ever did on earth. I'd also like to encourage you, whether you're sick or well, that God has a purpose for your life. Until we breathe our very last breath and pump out our final heartbeat, the game clock is still ticking for us to be playmakers for Christ!

My best friend Joe's little sister, Kristina, is like my own little sister. Because of our closeness, I've always considered her my sister, and she's always considered me her brother. Since middle school, Joe has been my best friend, and Kristina is only two years younger than us. Growing up, Joe and I were inseparable. We constantly spent the night at each another's houses, went on family vacations together and spent many holidays together. Momma Roxie, Papa Rome, and the Glovers were my second family and my home away from home.

It seems like yesterday; Kristina was finishing up her final year of schooling as a law student at Gonzaga University. She was working diligently toward becoming a judge and a teacher of justice and equality. I was so proud of her. I would describe Kristina as a girl with a heart of gold, relentlessly driven, guts and grit, a fitness junkie, possessing the strength of a lion, one who finishes strong, and one of the most unselfish and loving people I've ever been around.

In October of 2007, the unthinkable happened, as we received the most devastating news imaginable: Kristina had been diagnosed with stage-four ovarian cancer and was given six months to live. When I received the phone call, my heart dropped to floor and tears began streaming down my face. I remember praying, "No, God. No way. Not Kristina. This can't be possible! She's so young, Lord. She has the rest of her life in front of her. She's not done here on earth yet, Lord!" It felt like the world "went on mute." I was lost inside my own mind, struggling with God, pleading with God, reasoning with God. I was in shock and disbelief, and I felt like the world had literally come to a screeching stop. Because it had. Our world had. At this point, nothing else mattered except Kristina.

And the battle began. Let me rephrase that: The war began. There were surgeries, prayer sessions, chemo sessions on top of more prayer sessions and chemo sessions. We read Scripture over her, laid hands on her, and anointed her with oil. We had faith and believed God for healing. We placed her on every church prayer chain we had connections to. But nothing was working. And nothing did work. Kristina was eternally healed and went to be with Jesus not six months later, but four.

I don't know why bad things happen to good people. I don't know all the reasons why Kristina left us so early in life, and I don't know all the reasons why she had to die, of all things, from *cancer*. But I do know *one* reason: Kristina taught *me* more lessons about living *and* dying that I never would have learned otherwise. She taught me how you get through what you're going through, how to stand strong and finish strong, how to live unselfishly, and how to use my *hurts* to *help* other people.

You wouldn't believe the strength, courage, and perseverance Kristina possessed during those final four months. You wouldn't believe how unselfishly she lived and put everyone before herself. Not one time did she ever ask, "God, why me?" Not one time did she ever give up or stop fighting. And not one time did she ever stop giving and loving. She just kept on. She was well aware of her sickness, but even more aware of her purpose. Kristina's life mirrored the words of Paul, "to live is Christ, to die is gain" (Phil. 1:21, NIV).

It was surreal because as she became physically weaker, she became mentally, emotionally, and spiritually stronger. It was during those final four months that she ministered more to *us* than we ministered to *her.* And it was during those four months that I witnessed one of the most incredible, unselfish, and loving moments of my life. It was this very moment that redefined how I would live my own life of love and sacrifice.

Joe had a birthday. Kristina, physically feeble, pleaded with Momma Roxie and me to take her to the mall so she could buy her brother a birthday present. I told her that I didn't think it was a good idea, but Kristina would have it no other way. So there we were—Momma Roxie and I walking with our arms around Kristina through the mall in Spokane, Washington so that she could buy her brother a birthday present. That was Kristina. No excuses. No buts. No cancer or demon from the darkest pit of hell was going to stop that heart of gold from beating with love and purpose and giving her life away for the sake of others. No question, hell most certainly gave its best shot, but as the Bible says, "Love never fails" (1 Cor. 13:8, NIV).

I can't wait to see Kristina again! In the meantime, I know she's in good hands—God's hands, living a pain-free eternal life. I don't know why some people go sooner than later, but apparently, heaven needed Kristina's heart and couldn't go one more day without it.

If you or your loved one is suffering from terminal illness, I want you to know that my heart goes out to you. God loves you and has a purpose for you. Even if you're stuck in a hospital bed or in hospice, your life on earth still matters. Don't stop praying, dreaming, fighting, believing, or loving. God wants to use you.

BUT I'm Spiritually Hurting

Most people don't even realize they're spiritually hurting. And the most deadly and dangerous of pains are the ones you can't feel or the ones that sneak up on you and strike unexpectedly.

Pain serves as a warning light to the body, and if the warning light doesn't light up, danger is inevitable. In 2012, ABC News covered a story on a little girl who suffered from a rare and bizarre genetic disorder in which she cannot feel any physical pain. The disorder is extremely dangerous because the inability to feel pain means she may not be able to recognize a potentially deadly problem. For example, she would stick her hand in boiling water to pull out a utensil, not even realizing how badly she was burned. Crazy, right?!

The thing is, as bad as pain hurts, pain is God's gift to us, and is a warning light that something isn't right. King Solomon said it like this, "Sometimes it takes a painful situation to make us change our ways" (Prov. 20:30, GN). How many of you could preach a sermon on this verse?

Craving Pain

We all have a deep craving inside of us that longs to be fulfilled; we just don't always associate that crave with spiritual pain. Religious philosopher Blaise Pascal referred to the pain this way: "There is a God-shaped vacuum in the heart of every man which cannot be filled by any created thing, but only by God, the Creator, made known through Jesus." Our soul has a default sucking, pulling, drawing, craving that can only be satisfied in a relationship with God. We can try to stick the counterfeits of this world into our soul-vacuum, but it just leaves us empty and craving more.

According to tradition, there's a chilling illustration of how Eskimos used to kill wolves. First, the Eskimo would coat his razor sharp knife blade with dead animal blood and then allow it to freeze. Once frozen, he would then add several more layers of animal blood and ice until the blade was completely concealed by the frozen ice and blood. Next, the hunter would fix his knife handle into the ground with the sharp blade facing up. When a wolf would follow his sensitive nose to the source of the scent and discover the bait, he would lick through the first layer of ice and taste the fresh frozen blood. Yum! Excited, he'd begin to lick faster and faster through the layers, lapping the blade until the keen edge was bare. Feverishly, harder and harder, the wolf would lick the blade in the cold Arctic night. His craving for blood would become so great that he would not even notice the razor-sharp sting of the naked blade on his own tongue and that he was hemorrhaging; nor would he realize his insatiable thirst was being satisfied by his own warm blood. His carnivorous appetite would continue to crave more until in the morning light, the wolf was found dead on the snow.

Gruesome and unsettling, for sure! But it makes me think, that's exactly how our human sinful nature operates. We try to satisfy the appetites of our soul with the tantalizing lures the world has to offer such as power, position, prestige, pleasure, popularity, and possessions, all which leave us spiritually dead and decayed. These are what I call *joy decoys*. It's like trying to quench your thirst with salt water, or in the words of George Carlin, "trying to satisfy your hunger by taping sandwiches all over your body." It simply doesn't work. It leaves you empty, thirstier, and hungrier—and still craving for more. The only way to satisfy the craving hole in our soul is a relationship with Jesus Christ. Jesus said in the most famous sermon ever preached, the Sermon on the Mount, "Blessed are those who hunger and thirst for righteousness, for they will be filled" (Matt. 5:6, NIV).

Five Keys to Leaving the "BUT . . . I'm Hurting" Excuse behind You

It's time to get excited, because I'm here to tell you that God reigns over every pain! There's always hope for the hurting. And I want to inject five shots of hope deep into the depths of your soul, to help you put this *but* behind you—five injections that will keep *hurts and pains* from being the big but of your life. No buts, no excuses.

#1—Quench Your Spiritual Thirst

First things first: The first injection of hope is that God *can* heal your spiritual pain and quench your spiritual thirst. This is the starting point for everyone. The most exciting news in all of eternity is that God loves you and wants a relationship with you! There's only one way to be spiritually pain-free, and that is by being in a relationship with Jesus and allowing him to satisfy and quench the thirst of your soul. The psalmists said, "Oh, taste and see that the LORD is good! Blessed is the man who takes refuge in him" (Psalm 34:8, NIV); and "For He has satisfied the thirsty soul and the hungry soul He has filled with what is good" (Psalm 107:9, NASB).

If you've never allowed Jesus to quench your spiritual thirst by asking him be the Lord your life, I encourage you to do that right now. No buts, no excuses. Not tomorrow or next year; right now. Jesus said, "whoever drinks of the water that I will give him shall never thirst; but the water that I will give him will become in him a well of water springing up to eternal life. . . . I am the bread of life; he who comes to Me will not hunger, and he who believes in Me will never thirst" (John 4:13–14; 6:35, NASB)

Today is your day! If you haven't done so yet, it's time to surrender your life to Jesus! Paul said in Romans 10:9 (NIV), "If you declare with your mouth, 'Jesus is Lord,' and believe in your heart that God raised him from the dead, you will be saved." It's that simple!

If you'd like to satisfy your soul today by making Jesus Lord of your life, I invite you to pray this prayer with me:

Dear Jesus,

I invite you to be the Lord of my life. Today, I want to become a Christian. God, I ask you to satisfy my soul by filling me with your Holy Spirit. Thank you for dying on the cross for my sins and giving me a brand new life. You died for me, and now I am going to live for you, even if that means dying for you. Thank you, God, for filling the hole in my soul that is only designed for you. I love you. In Jesus' name, amen.

If you prayed that prayer just now, congratulations! You're a Christian! You just made the greatest and most important decision you will ever make in your life! How cool is that?

You know what else is cool? All of heaven is throwing a party right now—over *you*! Jesus said, "I tell you that in the same way there will be more rejoicing in heaven over one sinner who repents than over ninety-nine righteous persons who do not need to repent" (Luke 15:7, NIV). And here's our second injection of hope:

#2—Be Happy about Your Hurts

Preposterous, you might think? Well of course it is! And radically counterintuitive! I love what Wayne Dyer said, "If you change the way you look at things, the things you look at change." So true! The Bible teaches us to be happy about our hurts. Jesus' brother James said, "Consider it pure joy, my brothers and sisters, whenever you face trials of many kinds, because you know that the testing of your faith produces perseverance. Let perseverance finish its work so that you may be mature and complete, not lacking anything" (James 1:2–4, NIV).

No question, hurts and pains are trials of many kinds. We need to learn to consider them pure joy and to be happy about our hurts. Oftentimes, our hurting helps us more than our healing. Hurts keep us dependent on God, keep us compassionate toward others, and keep us thankful for every trying day we make it through. Paul said in 2 Corinthians 12:9b (PH), "I've cheerfully made up my mind to be proud of my weaknesses because they mean a deeper experience of the power of Christ in my life." Be happy about your hurts.

#3—Pray over Your Pains, and Be Prayed over for Your Pains

God heals! Pray the prayer Jeremiah prayed, "Heal me, O LORD, and I shall be healed" (Jer. 17:14, ESV). There's no hurt too big or too small that you can't take to the Lord. God cares about every single hurt. Whether you're in physical, emotional or spiritual pain—or all three at the same time—pray over your pains. Also, be prayed for. Check out what James 5:13–15 (NIV) says: "Is anyone among you in trouble? Let them pray. Is anyone happy? Let them sing songs of praise. Is anyone among you sick? Let them call the elders of the church to pray over them and anoint them with oil in the name of the Lord. And the prayer offered in faith will make the sick person well; the Lord will raise them up."

#4—Use Your Hurts to Help Others

People are hurting, and God desperately needs you to use your pain to help them! Remember, it's the model for us that Jesus set in motion. Again, there's never a pain in vain. If you've been hurt deeply *by* others, you can hurt deeply *with* others. When you're in pain, pray for someone else who is in pain. Get your mind off yourself! Shoot them a text message, send a card, call them, and let them know that you're praying for them and that you love them.

It's remarkable how love can penetrate straight past our pains and into our hearts. There's nobody better qualified to minister to someone else's pain than someone who's been in pain or is in pain. Use your hurts to help others.

And the fifth injection of hope is to always remember this:

#5—It's by the Thorn, Dependency Is Born

No matter the level of agony of your hurt or pain, you're going to make it. You're going to get through because God's got you! God's grace is sufficient for you, and his power is made perfect in your weakness.

Keep in mind that by the thorn, dependency is born. It's the thorn that reminds me I am completely and wholeheartedly dependent on God. Don't ever forget it. In fact, say it out loud: God, I depend on you.

God's grace will see you through and God's grace will heal you. Oftentimes we are just looking at God healing us through the wrong set of lenses. We want comfort. God wants character. We want freedom. God wants faith. We want easy. God wants everything. We want to feel good. God wants us to feel God. It's by the thorn, dependency is born. Your pain can actually heal you, because your pain can make you whole. Your pain can draw you closer to Jesus. Your pain is anointing you to serve Jesus, and to serve those around you. Take joy in that.

CHAPTER THREE

BUT . . . WHAT WILL PEOPLE THINK?

*All the while you're worrying about what people might be think-
ing about you, they are worrying about what you might thinking
about them!*

*Am I now trying to win the approval of human beings, or of
God? Or am I trying to please people? If I were still trying to
please people, I would not be a servant of Christ.*

Galatians 1:10, NIV

Ask yourself this question: What motivates you? What drives you?
Maybe you're not even totally certain, but these are critical questions to ask yourself and even more critical to find the answers to.
Whatever it is that drives you shapes every single decision you make
in your life.

There are countless motivating factors that can shape our lives.
The desire for power, possessions, prestige, or pleasure can drive
us, or even the desire to please God or please people. The driving
factors of our lives determine how we live our lives. The scary thing
is that if you're driven by the wrong motives, you'll either drive
yourself crazy or drive yourself off a cliff! That's why a little self-
examination about what motivates us is critical.

What Are People Thinking?

One of the most dangerous motivators that will drive you insane is
the constant worry about what people *might* be thinking about you.

If you find yourself constantly obsessing about what other people *might* be thinking about you, or you find yourself drumming up and dreaming up scenarios in your mind about thoughts they *might* be having about you, then chances are good you care way too much about what people think.

Notice my intentional use of the words "might," "might," and "might." Because the reality is: More than likely, they're *not* thinking about you! In fact, I've discovered that all the while you're worrying about what people might be thinking about you, they are worrying about what you might be thinking about them!

Worrying about what people think is a sure-shot way to cripple your life and severely impair the God-sized dream He has for you. Imagine what a big fat *but* we'd all have if we were stopped short of the Promised Land for our lives because of what other people *might be* thinking about us. Ludicrous! And frankly, always thinking about what others might be thinking is dangerously destructive for your life! Solomon said, "It is dangerous to be concerned with what others think of you, but if you trust the Lord, you are safe" (Prov. 29:25, GNT).

Why Do You Care, Anyway?

Have you wondered why you care what people think? That question, and its answer, is the starting point to kicking this *but* out of the way. So, why *do* you care? Why do you give a rip about what people think about you? Far too often, we live our lives a certain way because of what other people might think. I like how Edward Norton puts it in the movie Fight Club, "We buy things we don't need with money we don't have to impress people we don't even like." Why do we do that? The answer is because we care too much about what people think.

I want to give you two words that will set you free: Who. Cares? Peter, Jesus' disciple, cared what people thought, and one might argue for a good reason. Remember, he denied Christ *three times*! If the servant girl and the man who questioned him had thought that he really *was* Peter, he too would have been murdered. Sure we can all act like Peter had feeble faith and maybe so, but I've personally never been faced with a life-or-death situation while watching my closest friend and leader face execution (well, I've actually never faced a life-or-death situation, period). I mean, come on! If anyone deserved a pass for caring what people thought, wouldn't it have been Peter? Jesus was about to be murdered, and Peter would've been too! But he *didn't* get a pass, because no one gets a pass. Peter's faith was low and his fears were high—which are the two necessary ingredients for human insecurity. Listen to the story:

> Then they seized him and led him away, bringing him into the high priest's house, and Peter was following at a distance. And when they had kindled a fire in the middle of the courtyard and sat down together, Peter sat down among them. Then a servant girl, seeing him as he sat in the light and looking closely at him, said, "This man also was with him." But he denied it, saying, "Woman, I do not know him." And a little later someone else saw him and said, "You also are one of them." But Peter said, "Man, I am not." And after an interval of about an hour still another insisted, saying, "Certainly this man also was with him, for he too is a Galilean." But Peter said, "Man, I do not know what you are talking about." And immediately, while he was still speaking, the rooster crowed. And the Lord turned and looked at Peter. And Peter remembered the saying of the Lord, how he had said to him, "Before the rooster crows today, you will deny me three times." And he went out and wept bitterly (Luke 22:54–62, NIV).

Low faith, high fears, and Peter's worries led him to deny that he even knew Christ—not once, but three times: 1) "Woman, I do not know Him." 2) "Man, I am not." 3) "Man, I do not know what you are talking about." Low faith and high fears *always* lead to an insecure life full of regrets and disappointments.

I'm Insecure

If you're insecure, welcome to the human race! We all are. But just because we have insecurities, that doesn't mean they should have us. In fact, God wants to transform our insecurities into securities!

Within the definition of the word *insecure* we find other descriptives: unstable, uncertain, lacking confidence, shaky, unsound. When we are insecure, our emotions and abilities to make decisions are shaky and unstable, and our confidence levels are anything but level. If your life is built on insecurities, your life is built on instabilities. And a life that's insecure is a life that's unstable. Trying to build your life upon the foundations of insecurities would be like trying to build a house of cards during the middle of a massive earthquake! Both will crumble before they even get started.

On the flip side, within the definition of the word *secure* we find descriptive words like safe, stable, certain, firmly fastened, reliable, free from danger, attack, and risk of life. That's exactly the life we want and what God wants for us: a safe, stable, and secure life centered upon the foundation of Christ.

Unfortunately, there are many contributing factors that lead to an insecure life: poor body image, being rejected, never being accepted, failure or defeat, broken homes, and feeling overshadowed by people we think are smarter, nicer looking, or wealthier. These are all culprits of insecurities, right? And many of our insecurities are self-inflicted because we are constantly sizing ourselves up against other people.

The Compare Snare

Let me give you one of life's greatest secrets: Never compare. Comparing never works out to our benefit. Never, ever, *ever* compare yourself to others—it's a *sin snare*!

Let's face it, most of American society is engaged in "compare warfare." And the struggle is real. You compare yourself to me and I compare myself to you! We compare ourselves to our coworkers, colleagues, classmates, business persons, actors and actresses, and to the most beautifully airbrushed and photoshopped models alive. When we were kids we compared who got the coolest Christmas present, who the best athlete was, and who had the toughest daddy. (By the way, I always thought my daddy could whoop anybody's daddy. And he's only 5'5"!) As adults, the comparing continues. It's about who rocks the richest name brands, who has the hottest house, and who rolls in the most ridiculous ride. But the problem with all of this is that comparing yourself to others simply slaughters your self-esteem. When you compare yourself to others, one of two things happen: You think more of yourself, or you think less of yourself. Both are sinful. That ever-so-alluring temptation to compare yourself to others baits you into a hook, line, and emotionally sunk life!

Comparing either puffs you up or puts you down. I love how Pastor Steven Furtick said it, "The reason we struggle with insecurity is because we compare our behind-the-scenes with everyone else's highlight reel." Comparing will spin your life into a tail-chasing frenzy of insecurity and inferiority. Check out what the psalmist said in Psalm 73:2-3 (GNT), "But I had nearly lost confidence; my faith was almost gone because I was jealous." If you're constantly sizing yourself up, you'll be constantly sizing yourself down. Never compare. Never compare. Never, ever, ever compare—it's a sin snare.

Be You

Let's keep it real: Comparing yourself to others is like a slap in the face to the amazing God who created you. You are unique! Psalm 139 says God fearfully and wonderfully created *you!* Think about that for a minute. There are seven billion people on earth whom God created. Seven billion! But he only created one of *you*. One.

You are unique, and God desperately needs you to be *you*; the world desperately needs you to be *you*; and *you* desperately need you to be *you*. Don't be a counterfeit or a carbon copy of anybody; be yourself. You must be confident and comfortable in your own skin because God custom created you to be *you*!

I love what my five-year-old daughter Jazzlyn said to my wife Natalie one day. Jazzy is African American and she told my wife, "Mommy, I'm so happy I'm brown!"

Mommy said, "Me too, Jazzy! But why do you say that, sweet girl?"

"Because at school today I spilled hot chocolate on my face and you can't even see it because I'm camouflaged." Ha!

Hey, just like Jazzy, you need to be confident and comfortable in your own skin and in being *you*!

Be Your Best

Be the best *you* that *you* can be. Instead of setting your standard and measuring stick against the lives of others, set your standard against God's Word for your life. Paul said, "Let everyone be sure to do his very best, for then he will have the personal satisfaction of work done well and won't need to compare himself with someone else" (Gal. 6:4, LB). How cool is that!? Again, don't compare yourself with someone else.

I've had the privilege of spending the last twelve years ministering to professional athletes. I've led hundreds of chapel services inside NBA and MLB arenas and stadiums, and if I could summarize all twelve years of my messages into one theme it would be this, "Play for an audience of one." Play like Jesus is the only one in the arena sitting courtside at the half court line, wearing your jersey, chanting your name, and clapping and cheering for *you*! How about *that* for motivation!

And life is no different. Whether you're a teacher, student, physician, pastor, missionary, business professional, professional mommy or daddy, loving husband or wife, or a great friend, be the best *you* that *you* can be *for God*. Don't compare yourself to others, play for an audience of one: Jesus. Colossians 3:23 (NLT) says, "Work hard and cheerfully at whatever you do, as though you were working for the Lord rather than for people." Don't you love that verse? He said, "for the Lord, rather than for people." The reality is, when you live your life for God, everyone else will reap the benefits, too.

Be God's Masterpiece

God is the only One in the world you need to please—whom you *must* please. And you can't please both God and people! It's vital that our security be established upon whose we are and not who we are, and who the Word says we are and not who the world says we are.

What does God say about you? He says, "we are God's masterpiece. He has created us anew in Christ Jesus, so we can do the good things he planned for us long ago" (Ephesians 2:10, NLT). How awesome is that? You are God's masterpiece! A masterpiece is the greatest work of an artist, and that's exactly who you are! You're God's greatest work! David said in Psalm 139:13–14 (NIV), "For you created my inmost being; you knit me together in my mother's womb. I praise you because I am fearfully and wonderfully made; your works are wonderful, I know that full well." You are God's masterpiece. His works are wonderful, and you are God's fearfully and wonderfully created! So go ahead and "give yourselves completely to God" (James 4:7a). Be God's masterpiece!

Pleasing People? Please Don't.

Always worrying what people other people might be thinking can lead to the dangers of people-pleasing. Pleasing people is like a dog chasing its tail: you run around in circles, look absolutely ridiculous doing it, it's completely exhausting, and impossible to accomplish. You know as well as I do that trying to please people isn't fun and that it can't be done.

Instead of trying to please people, please God. The apostle Paul had the right mentality when he said, "Am I now trying to win the approval of human beings, or of God? Or am I trying to please people? If I were still trying to please people, I would not be a servant of Christ" (Gal. 1:10, NIV). Be a servant of Christ. Please God, not people.

Pleasing God? Please Do!

Who cares what other people think? Live a life that's pleasing to God. The Bible is clear: We are to please God and please him only. Even Jesus said, "I only seek to please Him who sent me" (John 5:30, LB). Unapologetically live your life to please God. After all, pleasing God, reverence for God, and putting your security and trust in God are the keys to producing a confident life. "Blessed is the man who trusts in the Lord and has made the Lord his hope and confidence. He is like a tree planted along a river bank with roots reaching deep into the water, not bothered by the heat, nor worried by long months of drought it stays green and goes on producing fruit" (Jer. 17:7–8, LB).

Deep roots. Your life must be deeply rooted in Christ, so that when the heat burns you don't, and when the drought depletes, you don't. Unfortunately, many Christians are like tumbleweed Christians. A little breeze blows by and we end up tumbling down the road and find ourselves crushed underneath the tires of the devil's diesel. But not you! Because blessed is the man (and woman) who trusts in the Lord and has made the Lord his hope and confidence. "Reverence for the Lord gives *confidence* and security to a man and his family" (Prov. 14:26, GNT, emphasis added).

What Are You Thinking?

What *are* you thinking, anyway? I mean, *why* are you thinking about what other people are thinking? Proverbs 4:23 (GN) says, "Be careful how you think, your life is shaped by your thoughts." You become what you think.

And since your life is shaped by your thoughts, an extremely important question to ask yourself is this: "What shapes my thoughts?" There are countless thought-shapers that ultimately blossom into life-shapers. Thought-shapers include what we see, hear, read, and listen to. Thought-shapers like the Internet, television, radio, the movies we watch, the music we listen to, the articles we read, and the people we listen to all shape our lives!

We need to learn to think before we think, and to train our brain before there's pain. Is your brain well-trained or a runaway freight train? (I feel like Dr. Seuss!) Look, if you want to stop paying attention to what other people think, start paying attention to what *you* think. Some people don't think and some people under-think, but most other people overthink. Overthinking is the art of creating problems that never existed, don't exist, and probably never will exist. If you want to change your life you have to change the way you think. Like Paul said, "Do not conform to the pattern of this world, but be transformed by the renewing of your mind" (Rom. 12:2, NIV). The only way to for you to change your stinkin' thinkin' is to renew your mind. *Every sin and every win starts with a thought.* I get it; this is easier said than done. If you're anything like me, there are many times when my mind doesn't mind itself.

How *do* you renew your mind, anyway? Let me give you three ways: You renew your mind by inspecting, rejecting, and reflecting. Simply put, you inspect what's in there, reject what shouldn't be, and reflect on what should be. I'm not suggesting you go into spiritual quarantine and completely isolate yourself from the world. Rather, I'm suggesting you completely insulate yourself from the world. If you're going to master what you grow, you're going to have to master what you sow. That means becoming a student of what seeds you plant, what seeds you allow to be planted, and what people you allow to plant them. Filter your minds! Inspect, reject, and reflect.

Guard Your Heart

The Bible is so relevant and practical it actually tells us what to think about: "Finally, brothers, whatever is true, whatever is noble, whatever is right, whatever is pure, whatever is lovely, whatever is admirable—if anything is excellent or praiseworthy—think about such things" (Phil. 4:8, NIV). But it doesn't stop with our heads. Again, Proverbs 4:23 (GNT) says, "Be careful what you think, your life is shaped by your thoughts." Interestingly enough, this same verse reads like this in the New International Version: "Above all else, guard your heart, for everything you do flows from it."

Guard your heart like your life depends on it! Because it does! The heart is the centerpiece of your life and the centerpiece of everything that lives. In Hebrew, the heart means the "kernel of the nut." And when the Bible instructs you to "guard your heart," it's talking about your minds, your feelings, your will, and your intellect. Why all the importance about the heart? Because if the devil can get to your heart, your life will fall apart. So above all else, guard your heart.

Piranhas vs. Nemo

I recently watched a video of five bloodthirsty piranhas devouring a helpless goldfish inside of a fish tank. (Don't ask me *why* I watched it; I guess my mind is pretty jacked-up, too!) Nevertheless, I watched these piranhas strategically, methodically, and patiently chip away at their prey. It was both captivating and creepy at the same time.

I happen to like goldfish. My daughter Jazzlyn is bananas over Nemo, which also means I am bananas over Nemo! Nemo's like a family member in my house. And when I was watching the above video, all I could think of was: Neeeeeeemoooo!

Well, check this out: The piranhas followed behind the goldfish diligently chipping away at his vulnerable caudal fin. The caudal fin is what fish use for propulsion. It's the motor that keeps the fish in locomotion. Without it, they sink. Since the goldfish was stuck in the tank and had nowhere to go, it swam frantically as fast as it could go back and forth and forth and back across the tank. But the piranhas just kept chipping and chipping until the entire caudal fin had been completely chewed off. And once the predators took the goldfish's caudal fin out, boom! The piranhas ate the goldfish *alive*!

Eerie! But this is exactly the strategy hell uses to prey on the human heart and mind. The enemy of our soul diligently tries to chip away at our minds, self-esteem, self-worth, and self-confidence—because he knows it will sink us. Just like the goldfish's caudal fin is the most important part of the fish's body to keep him safe and moving forward, the human heart and the human mind are the most important parts of the human body to keep us safe and moving forward. Without proper protection, the heart's left vulnerable, leaving us as a wide-open target to be eaten alive.

Above All Else

So there's good reason Solomon said, "above all else, guard your heart," because your life depends on it. Your heart is your lifeline. It's funny because people put endless amounts of efforts into guarding and protecting their most prized possessions. We have locks and alarms to protect our houses and cars; we have gated communities to protect our homes and families; we have pass codes to protect our identity and privacy; and we have a Department of Defense and a meticulously trained military that will do whatever it takes to protect our country. We educate ourselves, we spend whatever time or money it takes, and we will even put our own life in danger to protect our most prized possessions. But how far do we go to protect our hearts and minds? Do we even know how to guard and protect our hearts?

The Bible says, "In all circumstances take up the shield of faith, with which you can extinguish all the flaming darts of the evil one" (Eph. 6:16, ESV). The heart is to be guarded at all cost. Above all else, guard your hearts and guard your minds.

Unfortunately, many people treat their minds like tourist towns. Every and any thought is welcome to pass on through. They can come and go as they please, any time they want, and even move in and take up residence. But we need to treat our minds more like a fortified battle city! It's on lockdown. Nothing gets in without our permission! Thoughts need to be examined, filtered, and screened before we allow them to enter our minds and especially before we allow them to take up residence. And the only one who can approve what takes up residence in your mind is *you*.

If you're going to renew your mind and protect it, you're going to have to inspect, reject, and reflect what's in your mind.

From Least Mode to Beast Mode

In Judges 6–7 we find the powerful story of Gideon. He had insecurity and an inferiority complex. He struggled with inadequacy, low self-esteem, self-confidence, and self-doubt. His story is bonkers because he was a feeble, faith-challenged farm boy turned fearless, faith-filled national hero. Against absurd odds, he saved his nation.

Israel had hit rock bottom as a nation; the Bible tells us that they had done evil in the eyes of the Lord. They were economically, financially, emotionally, and spiritually bankrupt. And to add insult to injury, their land had been invaded and ravaged for seven years by 135,000 soldiers from their enemy nation, the Midianites. The Israelites were under such oppression that they were forced out of living in their own homes to living in caves. They desperately needed help, and they needed a courageous and confident leader they could rely on to rally the troops to deliver Israel. So God chose the opposite, Gideon:

> When the angel of the LORD appeared to Gideon, he said, "The LORD is with you, mighty warrior" (Jdgs. 6:12, NIV).

Mighty warrior?! Ha! Now that's funny! I can imagine Gideon thinking something like, "You've got to be kidding me! I'm no mighty warrior! I'm a mighty wimp!" But God had this outlandish plan of turning this chump into a champ. Gideon made up all sorts of excuses—check them out:

Excuse #1: *But* God, you got the wrong village! Wrong address, God! Gideon was born in Ophrah. Ophrah was a dinky, dusty village. Indeed, the name "Ophrah" actually meant "the town of dustiness"—not exactly a place you'd think a national hero would arise from.

Excuse #2: *But* God, you've got the wrong family! Our family is broke, like no joke! We're so broke we can't pay attention! We are the poorest family in our tribe! God, I don't even have the financial support and backing it would take to lead a military army into war!

Excuse #3: *But* God, you've got the wrong kid! I'm not the right person, Lord. I'm the youngest kid in my family! I'm the chump! You should choose someone older, wiser, with more experience. I'm too young to lead!

Thank God that *his* but is bigger than ours. Look what God says in Judges 6:23 (NIV): *"But* the LORD said to him, 'Peace! Do not be afraid. You are not going to die.'"* You see, God has a re*but*tal for every *but* we try to hide behind: "Peace! Do not be afraid." That is awesome! Not only was God giving His peace and comfort to Gideon, but two times, in verses 12 and 16, God gives Gideon his reassurance, "I will be with you"—the perfect words Gideon needed to hear in order to overcome his insecurities. God offered his peace, comfort, and reassurance that he was with Gideon and would keep him safe. And he offers the exact same thing for us!

The Pits

One of my greatest and most uplifting comforts is to know that any time I'm feeling inadequate, insecure, or inferior, God meets me right smack in the middle of my boohooing! Just like he met Gideon in the bottom of the dark pit of the winepress, he meets me in the darkest pits of my life, too. God is always a safe place when we're in a dark space. David said in Psalm 46:1–3 (MES):

"God is a safe place to hide, ready to help when we need him. We stand fearless at the cliff-edge of doom, courageous in sea storm and earthquake, before the rush and roar of oceans, the tremors that shift mountains."

No matter what inadequacies, insecurities, or inferiorities you might be going through, you can be secure because God is with you. So "be strong in the Lord and in the strength of his might" (Eph. 6:10, ESV). God is your strength and God is with you. "If God is for us, who can be against us?" (Rom. 8:31, NIV).

Spirit Clothes

Judges 6:34 (NIV) says: "Then the Spirit of the Lord came upon Gideon." The Hebrew means, "The Spirit clothed himself with Gideon." Incredible depiction! Spirit clothes? Come on somebody, get excited! Spirit clothes make you look better than Gucci, protect you better than combat gear, and comfort you better than your favorite pajamas.

After the roller-coaster conversation between God and Gideon, the Bible says, "Then the Spirit of the Lord came upon Gideon." God keeps his promises. Gideon now possessed the strength, confidence, and security to lead the charge. And Gideon did exactly that! Gideon's army of 300 took their weapons of mass destruction (torches, jars, and horns—because that's the way God rolls—His ways are not our ways) and faced off against 135,000 Midianite soldiers. Just the kind of odds God loves: 450 to 1! Horns, jars, and torches against armored soldiers with swords, daggers, spears, stones, slings, and bow and arrows! The perfect set-up for God to show up.

And in the middle of the night, Gideon and his undermanned band of 300 men made a complete circle throughout the valley as they blew their trumpets, shouted to God, broke their jars, and let their torches burn! What an approach to war! At any rate, the Midianites woke up in a panic. They heard the loud call of the war trumpet, the cracking noise of the jars breaking in the night, and saw the glow of the torches throughout the valley. God's approach made it look like the Midianites were up against thousands of heavily armed soldiers. And not knowing who was who, they started killing each other until every last one of them died. Go God.

If there's one thing I've learned in life, it's this: God plus one always equals a majority! God transformed Gideon from least mode to beast mode. You might feel like you're in the middle of a war that's battling against your thoughts of inadequacies, insecurities, and inferiorities, and that your odds of conquering them are 450 to 1. Well, I've got great news: Those are just the kind of odds God loves! It's the perfect set-up for God to show up! God doesn't want you to simply conquer; he wants you to be *more* than a conqueror! (Rom. 8:37). Let God be your security and remember: Whatever you aren't, God is! Whatever you don't have, God has! Wherever you are weak, he is strong!

Three Keys to Leaving the "BUT . . . What Will People Think?" Excuse behind You

#1—Root Your Confidence in Christ

Deeply root yourself in Christ and His love for you. No tumbleweed Christians! No buts, no excuses! Remember, you are *his* fearfully and wonderfully created masterpiece—His finest work! Who gives a rip about what anyone else thinks about you? So live like it! "In the fear of the Lord one has strong confidence" (Prov. 14:26, ESV).

#2—Be You. Be Your Best. Be God's.

Don't be a counterfeit or a carbon copy of anybody else. Be you, be the best *you* that *you* can be, and be God's! God loves you so much that he only created one of you. You are unique! Live your life to please God and to please God only. Play for an audience of one. He's wearing your jersey! He's chanting your name and he's clapping and cheering for *you*!

#3—Guard Your Heart

Protect your heart like your life depends on it—because it does. Renew your mind daily in the richness of God's Word! Your life is shaped by your thoughts, so be choosy about what shapes your thoughts. Inspect, reject, and reflect.

Great job for kicking that big but out of the way! Now, let's move on!

CHAPTER FOUR

BUT . . . MY AGE

Your age should never lock you in a cage.

Give yourselves completely to God—every part of you—for you want to be tools in the hands of God, to be used for His good purposes.

Romans 6:13, LB

Old as dirt or a little squirt—your age should never lock you in a cage. Obviously, the size of your *but* has nothing to do with how old or how young you are. Nonetheless, there seems to be an insecurity tactic the devil tries to use when it comes to our ages. Or maybe we shouldn't give the devil any credit at all; maybe *we* create the notion that age determines God's usability for our lives. We act as if there's a certain protocol for the age of usability. Many feel like they're too young, while others feel like they're too old. But you're never too young to get the dream done, and you're never too old to go for the gold!

But . . . I'm Too Young

In the Bible, age was a common *but* that people tried to hide behind. But if age were *any* factor in God's decision-making process for usability, the Bible wouldn't be imbedded with stories of people who defied the norms of age, both young and old. *Age* is not the three-letter word that decides if God can use you or not—*God* is. Whether your hearts have been beating for five years or one hundred years, your heart beats with a purpose. God wants to use you.

Take, for example, the life of Jeremiah. God asked Jeremiah—wait, let me rephrase: God *created and designed* Jeremiah—to serve as His prophet and to be his leader and mouthpiece. It was the very thing Jeremiah was created for, *but* when God asked him to serve as His prophet, Jeremiah didn't just give God one excuse, he gave him two: 1) I don't know how to speak; and 2) I'm only a boy. Look at the conversation oscillating back and forth between God and Jeremiah.

> The LORD spoke his word to me, saying: "Before I made you in your mother's womb, I chose you. Before you were born, I set you apart for a special work. I appointed you as a prophet to the nations." Then I said, "But Lord GOD, I don't know how to speak. I am only a boy." But the Lord said to me, "Don't say, 'I am only a boy.' You must go everywhere I send you, and you must say everything I tell you to say. Don't be afraid of anyone, because I am with you to protect you," says the LORD. Then the Lord reached out his hand and touched my mouth. He said to me, "See, I am putting my words in your mouth. Today I have put you in charge of nations and kingdoms. You will pull up and tear down, destroy and overthrow, build up and plant." (Jeremiah 1:5-10, NCV).

Can you imagine if you had missed the very call and purpose of what God created and designed you for because of a dumb excuse? Or even a good excuse? Jeremiah almost did. If you recall, Moses nearly did the same thing eight hundred years before this. In Exodus 4, God told Moses to go and tell the king of Egypt, "Let my people go!" To which Moses used the excuse, *but* God, "I can't speak well. I talk too slowly." Thankfully, God's encouragement and patience and plan for us is bigger than our *buts*.

Jeremiah was a mere seventeen years old when God called him to lead and he went on to become known as one of the major prophets (in fact, the last major prophet) in the Old Testament. He lived and led during the final days of the disastrous crumbling of the nation of Israel. The Israelites had drifted and become so hardened and calloused to their sins that they no longer believed or feared God. God called Jeremiah to be a mouthpiece to warn the Israelites to repent and turn back to God. Jeremiah ended up preaching God's love (and judgment) to the Israelites for forty years. He's been credited with authoring the books of Jeremiah, Lamentations, and possibly 1 and 2 Kings, all of which have been impacting millions of lives for thousands of years. Not bad for a seventeen-year-old boy who didn't think he knew how to speak.

Mind. Blown.

Here's a crazy story for you: When my daughter Kylie was only five years old (she's now fourteen), she led her teacher, Ms. Nirva, to the Lord! Wait, what?! She was only five! The way we found out was by Ms. Nirva telling the good news to my wife, Natalie. Mind. Blown. Ms. Nirva ended up attending our church services every week, getting water baptized, and getting plugged into a home group. Now *that's* amazing! Or is it? Shouldn't that be the norm—that one's age shouldn't dictate usability? Shouldn't *every* five-year-old be capable of leading their teacher to the Lord?

My twelve-year-old son's name is Josiah, named after King Josiah. Josiah was a complete rock star for God (and I might add, so is my son). He was the youngest king to ever reign—eight years old. He might have been little, but he was God's giant! He reigned as king for thirty-one years. Once again, amazing, right? Or, maybe, it's supposed to be normal?

The bottom line is that our age is never God's gauge for usability. How could God possibly use my five-year-old daughter Kylie to lead her teacher to the Lord? And how could God possibly use eight-year-old King Josiah to rule as king? Second Chronicles 34:1

(NIV) gives us the secret: "He did what was right in the eyes of the Lord . . . not turning aside to the right or to the left." God doesn't look at age; he looks at the heart and whether or not you're usable. In fact, "GOD is always on the alert, constantly on the lookout for people who are totally committed to him" (2 Chron. 19:9, MES).

Modern-Day Young Successes

There are more jaw-dropping stories of young people lighting the world on fire than can be accounted for, even in today's day and age. Everyone loves a great success story, right? Especially stories that defy the odds. When you think of young successes, it's easy to immediately think of Mark Zuckerberg who was a nineteen-year-old sophomore at Harvard who launched Facebook from his dorm room. But there are numerous other stories of young and successful modern-day inspirations. Take for example, preteen Luci Li. Luci, an eleven-year-old pro golf phenom, was the youngest player to ever qualify for the US Open and play against the best female golfers around the world

Or maybe you've heard of Nick D'Aloisio. Nick was a fifteen-year-old British programmer who wrote the mobile news summarization application Summly, from his parents' bedroom. Two years later, when he was seventeen, he sold it to Yahoo for $30 million dollars. Thirty mil! Then there's Stacey Ferreira, an eighteen-year-old who cofounded MySocialCloud along with her brother Scott. MySocialCloud is a secure website company that stores all your usernames and passwords all in one place—perfect for the great majority of people who are forgetful, unorganized, or just flat-out busy. And of course we're probably all familiar with the old-school success stories of then-young men like Steve Jobs and Bill Gates who founded Apple and Microsoft at age twenty-one, or Michael Dell who started the Dell computer company at nineteen years old. Young guns!

If you're young, I encourage you to use your energy, enthusiasm, and fearless creative efforts to set the world on fire! The Bible says in 1 Timothy 4:12 (GWT), "Don't let anyone look down on you for being young. Instead, make your speech, behavior, love, faith, and purity an example for other believers." Young person, lead the way! Go ahead, set the world ablaze!

But . . . I'm Too Old

Feeling old? As Bob Hope said, "You know you're getting old when the candles cost more than the cake." And there's another saying, "If things get better with age, then I'm approaching magnificent!"

That would describe my Grandpa Hearn—magnificent! Grandpa is eighty-three. He has one of the most fun personalities of anyone I know. He's jolly, playful and boy does grandpa got jokes! Years ago, he proudly wore a hat around in public that read, "I'm not old, just a recycled teenager." And I think Grandpa truly believes that. He's young at heart and in spirit. Sure, his body might have aged, but his mind is still young. He has a different way of viewing the aging process and he seems to enjoy it. Instead of fighting it, he seems to invite it.

Still, to this day, at eighty-three years old, Grandpa works around the house, building steps, laying down wood floors, and working on cars; whatever his hand finds to do, his hands do it. Mark Twain once said, "Age is a matter of mind over matter. If you don't mind, it doesn't matter." And to Grandpa, it doesn't matter.

Solomon said, "The glory of young men is their strength, but the splendor of old men is their gray hair. Gray hair is a crown of glory; it is gained in a righteous life" (Prov. 20:29; 16:31, ESV). I hope this verse makes you look at your gray hair differently. If you have some gray color going on—what a blessing! Gray hair is cool like shade; it's the new trend, a crown of wisdom, splendor, and glory!

According to USNews.com, thirteen percent of the American population is sixty-five years and older. Thirteen percent is a large slice of the American pie! And gallup.com states that the average American retires at sixty-two years old. But no matter how old you get, or what age you decide to retire from work, you never retire from *God's* work. In fact, the older we get, the more tools we have in our toolbox! God doesn't look at age, he looks at usability. The question is not, "Am I too old?" The question is, "Am I usable"? God wants to use you, so make sure you're usable. "Give yourselves completely to God—every part of you—for you want to be tools in the hands of God, to be used for His good purposes" (Rom. 6:13, LB).

One of the greatest inspirations in my life is a woman named Louise Simonsen. Louise is ninety years old. During my Bible school days, I lived with Louise and her wonderful husband Bob, who has since gone to be with our Lord. Bob and Louise were my host family. They took me in like I was their own child, provided me with a room, fed me, and most importantly encouraged me in my daily walk with Jesus Christ. Louise is an incredible woman of God who has never allowed her age to stop her from giving Jesus to the world. In fact, today she leads five church services per week within various assisted living homes. What a ministry! She takes church to people who can't get to church. The crazy thing is, she's older than many of the people who live in these homes. She also holds a nightly devotional over the phone with friends whom she is discipling and mentoring. And last but not least, she's a prayer warrior. This woman can pray down the heavens.

It's fascinating to think about, but I would not be where I am today with God if not for Bob and Louise. They were so instrumental in my walk and growth in God that, perhaps, without their influence in my life, I might not even have become a pastor. I pray that one day, I will grow old to be just like Louise.

Other Oldies-but-Goodies

Two of my lifelong friends and mentors are Duane and Melvin Middleton. I became a Christian under their ministry. Duane and Melvin are brothers and these guys have an incredible family. Their dad's a pastor, their grandpa was a pastor, their grandpa's grandpa was a pastor, and so on—I'm pretty sure their family bloodline dates back to Jesus! Years ago, when Duane and Melvin's mom, Lavinia was sixty-four, she decided to do something ridiculously insane for Jesus—and while I know sixty-four is the new forty-four, this is flat crazy. In efforts to help raise money for missionaries, she would get as many people as she could to pledge money toward the mission if she . . . jumped out of an airplane and skydived! And she did just that. The money came in and Lavinia jumped out! She had never skydived before in her life! I remember watching the video of her inspirational jump; she was brave, smiling, spinning, and most importantly, *doing God's work. That* is amazing.

Several years ago, the Phoenix Suns introduced a new halftime routine that they perform a couple times throughout the season—the Golden Grannies. It is so much fun and absolutely hysterical! The first time I watched them I laughed so hard my face hurt! As halftime starts, thirty-two gray-haired grannies hit the hard wood floor and get their dance on. The crowd erupts with cheers and laughter as the grannies groove to some of the most groovin' and recognizable music on the radio. You should see those grannies whip, nae nae, and turn around and drop it like it's hot! It just goes to show that you're never too old to be a Suns dancer.

And then there's Desiline Victor. Desiline was coined by Reader's Digest as a voting legend. And she was. At the ripe old age of usability, 102 years old and in a wheelchair, she sat in line for several hours waiting to vote at her Florida polling station. Her dedication to vote was so inspiring that it caught the attention of President Obama, who acknowledged her in his State of the Union. Desiline now has a bill named after her that will ease the voting process for people in the future called "Desiline's Free and Fair Democracy Act." Rock on, Desiline!

Ninety Years Old and Pregnant

Yes, you read that right—because *nothing* is impossible with God. I love the story in Genesis 18: The Lord appeared to Abraham by sending three men (probably angels) near some trees while

Abraham was sitting at the entrance of his tent. As God began to talk with Abraham through these men, his wife Sarah overheard the entire conversation. Verse 10 says, "Then one of them said, 'I will surely return to you about this time next year, and Sarah your wife will have a son.'" Sarah about fell out! Verse 12 (NIV) says, "she laughed to herself as she thought, 'After I am worn out and my lord is old, will I now have this pleasure?'"

Sarah's probably thinking to herself, now *that's* funny, God, that's a good one! But it almost felt like a bad joke. The one thing Sarah desired more than anything in life was a child. From the very moment she married Abraham, she longed to have children. But she never could. She was barren throughout her normal childbearing years, and in fact, that's essentially the first thing the Bible states about Sarah: "Now Sarai was childless because she was not able to conceive" (Gen. 11:30, NIV). And now that I'm ninety years old and my husband is one hundred years old, God is telling us we're gonna have a baby?! *Riiiiight.* But watch what happens next:

> Then the LORD said to Abraham, "Why did Sarah laugh and say, 'Will I really have a child, now that I am old?' Is anything too hard for the LORD? I will return to you at the appointed time next year, and Sarah will have a son." And once again, God kept his promise because that's exactly what God does! "Now the LORD was gracious to Sarah as he had said, and the LORD did for Sarah what he had promised. Sarah became pregnant and bore a son to Abraham in his old age, at the very time God had promised him. Abraham gave the name Isaac to the son Sarah bore him (Gen. 21:1–2, NIV).

And that's the moral of this story: *Nothing* is impossible with God. He always keeps his promises. No matter how young or how old you are, your age doesn't lock you in a cage. God refuses to be limited or restricted from His miracles and purposes for your life because of how old you are or aren't. No matter the amount of years you've lived, if you still have a dream—go after it! Keep the very words of Jesus at the forefront of your mind, "For nothing is impossible with God" (Luke 1:37, NIV).

Go ahead. I dare you. Chase your God-sized dream and watch God do the impossible! God would tell you that he can do infinitely more in your life than anything you could ever ask or imagine—and does! Look at it: "Glory belongs to God, whose power is at work in us. By this power he can do infinitely more than we can ask or imagine" (Eph. 3:20, GWT).

So let's start asking, and let's start imagining, and then watch him do infinitely more! Whether you're young or old, you're the perfect age for God to use you—today!

Titus 2 Types of Old Folk

In the second chapter of Titus, Pastor Titus lays it down for the older men and women. His message? Forever inspire, and never retire.

> Guide older men into lives of temperance, dignity, and wisdom, into healthy faith, love, and endurance. Guide older women into lives of reverence so they end up as neither gossips nor drunks, but models of goodness. By looking at them, the younger women will know how to love their husbands and children, be virtuous and pure, keep a good house, be good wives. We don't want anyone looking down on God's Message because of their behavior. Also, guide the young men to live disciplined lives" (Titus 2:2–6, MES).

Titus gives seven directives to the older men: live lives of temperance, dignity, wisdom, healthy faith, love, endurance, and guide the young men to live disciplined lives. In this same chapter (v. 3–5),

Titus delivers similar instructions for older women. Only this time, he gives the women eight instructions (a clear indicator that women need more instruction than men do—I'm kidding! Don't hate!). But these eight instructions are words of encouragement for the older ladies to set the example for the younger ladies. Titus said: live a life of reverence, don't be a gossip, don't be a drunk, be a model of goodness, be virtuous, pure, keep a good house, and be good wives. Part of God's plan for your life, as you get older, is that he wants you to be an example and set the standard for godly living as you minister to the younger generations.

Do as I Say, Not as I Do

When I was a kid, there were some adults in my life who used questionable language and even had questionable behavior—and I was watching. They'd glance my way and sort of chuckle and say, "Travis, do what I say, not what I do." And what would I do? I did what they *did*; because that's what we do!

Do as you say and not what you do? Gimme a break! What a spineless excuse of a coward to hide behind for bad living! The real saying should be, "Do as I do *and* as I say" because the two should be in alignment and harmony. This is called *example*.

Whether you consider yourself young or old, never underestimate the power of the influence you have through living a godly life of example. People are watching. Paul throws a couple of powerful verses our way about being examples:

- "Follow God's example, therefore, as dearly loved children" (Eph. 5:1, NIV).
- "Follow my example, as I follow the example of Christ" (1 Cor. 11:1, NIV).

Make no mistake about it, the examples we set, whether good or bad, have copycat effects. Let me give you an *example*: I'm a pastor. I teach the Bible in front of my church congregation every single weekend. One day, when I came home from the office and walked into Kylie's room (she was four at the time), she had a bunch of her dollies and stuffed animals spread out on her bedroom floor and Kylie was preaching to them. That's an example of an example. Kylie watches Daddy, and Kylie copies Daddy. Example is power. Example is influence. And every last one of us possesses the power of influence—the power to lead by example.

Years ago, when I was mowing my lawn, my son Josiah (five at the time) ran over to the patio and grabbed his toy lawnmower. Josiah literally, for fifteen minutes, followed directly behind me pushing his toy mower, convinced he was cutting the grass just like Daddy. That's example. Josiah watches Daddy, Josiah copies Daddy.

We have a rule in our house for our kiddos about the language they use. I picked it up from one of my pastors, Pastor Duane, before my three kids were born, and maybe you'd like to implement it into your set of family rules as well. Here's the rule: If Mommy and Daddy say it, you can say it. It's a powerful rule. This not only sets an example for your kids to follow, but it holds you accountable to use words that you want your kids using.

So there you have it. We've successfully debunked the notion that one's age has anything to do with God's usability. And as we kick the age *but* out of our way, we forge ahead toward God's plan and purpose for lives. I'd like to remind you of three keys as we close out this chapter.

Three Keys to Leaving the "BUT . . . My Age" Excuse behind You

#1—Remember, Your Age Never Locks You in a Cage

Your age doesn't determine the size of your but. You're never too young to get the dream done, and you're never too old to go for the gold. Dare to dream and dare to live your dream. Defy the odds, so no one can deny it's God. Don't listen to what the devil tells you, don't listen to what society tells you, and please don't listen to what *you* tell you. Listen to the voice of God and go for the gold.

#2—Pray for God to Use You

Again, God is looking for usability. And let me just add that asking God to use you is one of the most dangerous prayers you can pray! Because if you dare ask, he will use you in ways you would have never dreamed possible. Be available, be reliable, and be pliable. "Give yourselves completely to God—every part of you—for you want to be tools in the hands of God, to be used for His good purposes" (Rom. 6:13, LB).

#3—Do As You Say *and* Say As You Do

No matter your age, never forget you have tremendous influence. People are watching. Be an example, be consistent, and be authentic. Set the bar of your life to the standard of the Bible, and live your life with deep conviction to follow God's Word and the example of Christ. "Follow God's example, therefore, as dearly loved children" (Eph. 5:1, NIV).

CHAPTER FIVE

BUT . . . I DON'T HAVE TIME

Never let the speed of life bleed your life of what matters most.
Live life with a due sense of responsibility, not as those who do not
know the meaning and purpose of life but as those who do. Make
the best use of your time, despite all the difficulties of these days.

Ephesians 5:15–16, PH

We live in the busiest generation in history. We are overscheduled, overworked, and overwhelmed! If you're not purposeful and protective about how you spend your time, the speed of life could bleed your life of what matters most. We hide behind the excuse way too often, *"BUT . . . I don't have time." But* the reality is: You *do* have time. In fact, you have plenty of time—the exact same amount of time as every other successful person who has ever lived. You have time for what you have time for.

Time Flies

It's crazy how fast time flies. My four-year-old Kylie just turned fourteen. My two-year-old Josiah just turned twelve. Our answer to ten years of prayer, Jazzlyn, is now five. Seriously, how did *that* happen?! I have no idea how my kids just flew through a decade at what seemed to be the speed of light, but they did! In fact, now that I'm thinking about it, how is it possible that I'm even a daddy? Yesterday I was blowing out four candles and today I'm lighting up fourteen candles.

In today's fast-paced society, everyone I know is running. We wake up. Jump out of bed. Get the kids off to school. Speed to work. Eat on the way. Pick up the kids from school. Hurry them over to practice. Eat on the way home. Crash into bed. Wake up and repeat the cycle. The bad news is time flies. The good news is: You're the pilot!

We live in such a fast-paced society that it's nearly impossible to slow down and enjoy the beautiful things in life that matter most. Slowing down in today's lightning-bolt society would be like trying to enjoy the impressive views of the Grand Canyon while flying overtop in a Lockheed SR-71 Blackbird Jet. Ever heard of one of those bad boys? Let me tell you, they are something to behold, an engineering marvel, and are lightning-fast with a typical cruising speed of Mach 3.2—more than 2,200 miles per hour! Bad. To. The. Bone.

Sorry for getting a little sidetracked, but I'm a guy and jets are cool. My point is—that's the life we live: rollin' like freight trains, flyin' like airplanes, and life in the fast lanes. It's a microwave society. We eat our food on the go, we hold our meetings on the drive, and we take our families on work-vacations. We're overscheduled and double-booked, all the while we're bragging about our eighty-hour work weeks. We act like multitasking is a trait to envy, when in reality it produces mediocre results.

We are sprinting after money and success at a faster pace than our legs can take us and at a faster speed that the world has ever seen. We don't stop, we don't pause, and we certainly don't slow down; we just keep running. And for me personally, sometimes in life I feel like I'm running downhill. It's a fine line between running faster than I've ever run and falling harder than I've ever fallen. But, why wouldn't I? And why wouldn't you? Isn't that's what society packages and promotes as success? Run. Fast. At any cost. Because you'll get trampled on and left behind if you don't.

It's hard for me to imagine Jesus' brother James saying, "What is your life? You are a mist that appears for a little while and then vanishes" (James 4:14, NIV). I mean, it's not hard for me to imagine our life is like a mist that quickly vanishes—it's just hard for me to imagine a guy who lived 2,000 years ago saying that! Seriously, think about how slow life must have seemed 2,000 years ago. Imagine, for a minute, life without cell phones, computers, video games, e-mail, Facebook, Instagram, Twitter, television, trains, planes, and automobiles! What the heck did they do? I can't even imagine driving five hours in a car without cell phones, iPads, or Kindles to keep my kids entertained! When I was a kid, I counted telephone poles and played slug bug for five hours! When Jesus was a kid, they probably rode by on their donkeys counting desert tortoises and fig trees for five hours! What I'm saying is, time flies; and in today's fast-paced life, it's more like flashing!

King Solomon said in Ecclesiastes 3:1 (NIV), "There is a time for everything, and a season for every activity under the heavens." That said, there might be a time for everything, but there's no way there's time for everything. That's why it's incredibly important to make the most of our time. David, Solomon's daddy, said, "Teach us to number our days and recognize how few they are. Help us to spend them as we should" (Ps. 90:12, LB).

Setting Priorities

One of my favorite time management passages from the Bible is Ephesians 5:15–16 (NIV): "Be very careful, then, how you live—not as unwise but as wise, making the most of every opportunity, because the days are evil." Don't you just love that verse? Be careful, be wise, and make the most of every opportunity. And every day that God gives you is exactly that—an opportunity!

Making the most of every opportunity is going to demand that you set priorities for your life. Setting priorities is a common principle in time management. It's funny, but there are many popular time-management phrases we use that aren't even humanly possible. For example we say things like save time, make time, or manage time. The truth is, you can't *save* time and store it up for later, you can't *make* more time than has already been made, and you can't *manage* time because time keeps on tickin'. A.W. Tozer wrote: "Time is a resource that is nonrenewable and nontransferable. You cannot store it up, slow it up, hold it up, divide it up or give it up. You can't hoard it up or save it for a rainy day—when it's lost it's unrecoverable. When you kill time, remember that it has no resurrection."

Although you can't manage time, you can manage choices. And choice management is about setting priorities. Remember, time flies and you're the pilot! You have time for what you have time for. And *time* is the most valuable treasure God has given you. How are you spending it?

Let me ask the question this way: If your heart were to be buried in the place where you spent most of your time, where would it be buried? In your Bible? In your family? In your wallet? In your office? In front of the TV? Where is your heart? How do you spend your time?

Where you invest your time reveals what's most important to you. Ask yourself this question, "Where does my time go"? This may take some self-evaluation in order to figure out—which is fine, because God's Word tells us, "Look carefully at how you live! Live purposefully and worthily and accurately, not as the unwise but as wise, sensible, intelligent people" (Eph. 5:15, AMP). Do some self-evaluation. Slow down and look carefully at how you live. Once you know where your time is going, you can prioritize where you want it to go.

Big Rocks

I heard of a physics professor who was teaching his students about time management. He gave his students a wide-mouth mason jar, five big rocks, a handful of marbles, a container of sand and a glass of water. He said, "You've got fifteen seconds to put all of these items in the jar."

The physics teacher then stepped back with his stopwatch in his hand and yelled, "Go!" The students poured in the sand, tossed in the marbles and started stuffing the rocks in. After fifteen seconds he shouted, "Time's up." They had failed.

Still left sitting on the table were three large rocks and the glass of water. The students argued, "It can't be done. It's impossible. The jar is too small."

The teacher replied, "I will show you how to put them all in the jar." He took the jar and placed a couple of the big rocks in the jar. He filled in any gaps around the big rocks with the marbles and continued to fill the jar until it was up to the brim with all the big rocks and all the marbles. The teacher then took the sand and slowly poured it into the jar and watched as it cascaded around the rocks and the marbles – filling all the holes and spaces. He then took the glass of water and poured it into the jar. Voila! Everything fit perfectly. He then said, "It all fits— but it depends on the order that you put them in the jar—and that is a matter of setting priorities. When your priorities are in order, you can make them all fit."

Put your biggest rocks in the jar first! And the biggest Rock, as we all know, is Jesus Christ.

God's Time

God must always be first. God is priority number one! Of course, we already know this. It's certainly head information, but is it heart transformation?

Jesus, "The Sermonator," preached the mess out of the concept of keeping our priorities in check in Matthew 6. And I mean *he brings it*, as he goes straight after the self-seeking heart of man. His sermon consisted of brilliant teachings such as: don't broadcast to the world when you give, don't pray or fast like the hypocrites do, and don't store up for yourselves earthly treasures; rather, store up for yourselves heavenly treasures. In short: Don't seek money or recognition; seek God. As he said in verse 24 (NIV), "No one can serve two masters. Either you will hate the one and love the other, or you will be devoted to the one and despise the other. You cannot serve both God and money." In life, you're always chasing something. You're running after something. And you can't run in two different directions at the same time—it just can't be done.

Then, in the grand finale, Jesus lights up the sky with faith fireworks: "But seek first his kingdom and his righteousness, and all these things will be given to you as well" (Matt. 6:33, NIV). Don't worry about the future, Jesus says; God's got you! Let's break this verse down a little bit:

- *"But"*, which means *instead* or *in lieu* of "self" ... instead of seeking all the worldly desires of the flesh ...
- *"Seek"*—search, locate, discover, to go toward, to pursue ...
- *"His kingdom and his righteousness"*—Instead, seek God, his work, his mission, and his holiness.

In other words: Instead of pursuing your own self-seeking, self-serving desires, seek and pursue God, his work, his mission and his holiness. Seek God first—in fact, solely—and let him take care of the rest.

Let's face it, we already know that God is supposed to take first place, but all too often God is misplaced or displaced in our lives. And we also know that anything that is "out of order" is broken and doesn't work. Typically, when things are "out of order" in life, we fix them. If God is not first place in your life, your life is broken, it's out of order, and needs to be fixed. Making God first doesn't simply mean making God the first moment of our day; it means making God the first moment of *every* moment of our day.

The bottom line is that if God is first place in your *life*, he will also be first place in your *time*. I invite you to take a minute to perform the following brief self-evaluation. These five questions are simply for you to evaluate whether or not God is taking first place in your life. I encourage you to slow down, take your time, and prayerfully and carefully answer these questions. (Don't cheat! I won't look at your answers, I promise!)

1. Do I read my Bible *daily*?
   - What time? For how long?
   - Do I study God's Word? How often?
   - Do I memorize God's Word? How often?
   - Do I share God's Word? How often?

2. Do I pray *daily*?
   - What time(s)?
   - For how long?
   - All throughout the day?
   - What do I pray about?

3. Do I give God my praise and worship *daily*?
   - If yes, prove it to yourself by thinking of examples.

4. Does my bank account reflect that God is first?
   - Do I tithe ten percent of my gross income to my local church?
   - Am I consistent?
   - Do I give above and beyond my tithe to missions and other ministries?

5. Do my closest friends reflect that God is first in my life?
   - Name them.

The answers to these questions should give you an idea of whether or not you're spot-on, need some improvement, or need some major improvement! Whatever your results, God wants your time and wants to be first place in your life. First place was designed for Him. In fact, he desires this so much that it's the first of the Ten Commandments: You shall have no other gods before me.

Sure, this commandment includes not having false gods from the Bible like Baal, Baal-Zebub, Dagon, and golden calves, but it also includes the false gods in our lives like our time, talent, and treasures. The bottom line is: Anything that takes first place in our lives can be considered a *god* that we put before God.

The Bible also tells us that God is a jealous God. "You shall not make for yourself an image in the form of anything in heaven above or on the earth beneath or in the waters below. You shall not bow down to them or worship them; for I, the LORD your God, am a jealous God" (Ex. 20:4–5, NIV). God loves you dearly and desires to have first place in your life. So let's keep him where he belongs—first!

And let's also not forget the fourth commandment: "Remember the Sabbath day, to keep it holy." This consecrates the first day of every week to God. The crazy thing is that if we're not setting aside an entire day out of our week as a sabbath day for God, not only are we out of order, but we are breaking one of God's ten commandments. Whoa!

> Observe the Sabbath day, to keep it holy. Work six days and do everything you need to do. But the seventh day is a Sabbath to God, your God. Don't do any work - not you, nor your son, nor your daughter, nor your servant, nor your maid, nor your animals, not even the foreign guests visiting in your town. For in six days God made Heaven, Earth, and sea, and everything in them; he rested on the seventh day. Therefore God blessed the Sabbath day; he set it apart as a holy day. (Ex. 20:8–11, MES)

Family Time

The next biggest rock must be your family. D.L. Moody said, "A man ought to live so that everyone knows he's a Christian; and most of all, his family ought to know." I am a family guy. I love my family, and family time is my favorite time next to God's time. My family started more than seventeen years ago when I married the love of my life, Natalie. Together, she and I made up the Hearn family. A family of two. She's my best friend to this day. I love being with my wife and doing life with her. I know there are those married couples who live under the same roof together, yet live two separate lives; but that's not Natalie and me. We do just about everything together. I love going out on dates my wife, talking with my wife, laughing with my wife, shopping with my wife, hiking with my wife, working out with my wife, and just sitting back and relaxing and watching a good movie with my wife. As our marriage has progressed throughout the years, our family has grown as God brought three amazing kiddos into our lives—now we're a family of five!

I also cherish my time with my kids! I enjoy coaching my kids, playing ball with my kids, swimming with my kids, wrestling around and being silly with my kids. I am crazy about my family and I thank God for my family. And aside from God, my family comes first. And I know yours does, too!

Once again, time flies and *you're* the pilot. You get to choose what's first, second, third, and twenty-third. Either you control your calendar, or your calendar controls you. Family *always* comes before career, money, and even ministry—and let me tell you something, you'll have to fight for it. Life is demanding. Careers are demanding, and people are demanding. But, seriously, what good would it be to have a successful career or even ministry if your family is neglected or is falling apart? Spending time with God and your family are the two single most important time-management *choices* you can make. If you spend your time on nothing else other than God and family, you've spent your time wisely.

Time for My Spouse

God invented family. Family is *his* idea. And the Bible offers enormous amounts of wisdom and guidance for families. In Chapter 2 of the very first book of the Bible, God begins to orchestrate the first family and lay down the importance family time. Let's look at it:

> The LORD God said, "It is not good for the man to be alone. I will make a helper suitable for him. So the LORD God caused the man to fall into a deep sleep; and while he was sleeping, he took one of the man's ribs and then closed up the place with flesh. Then the LORD God made a woman from the rib he had taken out of the man, and he brought her to the man. The man said, "This is now bone of my bones and flesh of my flesh; she shall be called 'woman,' for she was taken out of man." That is why a man leaves his father and mother and is united to his wife, and they become one flesh. (Gen. 2:18, 21–24, NIV)

In this passage, Moses provides powerful and intimate imagery for the *oneness* of a family. The first family started out with a man, and a woman formed from out of the man. He uses phrases like "not good for man to be alone," "I will make a helper for him," "God made a woman from the rib he had taken out of the man," "bone of my bone, flesh of my flesh," and "one flesh." All of these phrases point to the *oneness* of family and can only be produced through *one* word, time. Intimacy can only come through spending time together. The more time you spend with your spouse and kids, the more oneness. The less time you spend with your spouse, the less oneness. God made woman from the man's rib, she's now bone of his bone and flesh of his flesh, she's called "woman" (in Hebrew *isha*) and he is called man (In Hebrew, *ish*), and together, through marriage, they become one flesh. One faith. One flesh. One family. One.

Paul repeated these very words to the church in Ephesus: "A man leaves his father and mother and is joined to his wife, and the two are united into one. This is a great mystery, but it is an illustration of the way Christ and the church are one" (Eph. 5:31–32,

NLT). Spectacular! The oneness of marriage is an illustration of the way Christ and the church are *one.*

If you are married, clear your schedule to spend time with your spouse today. Nothing, aside from your time with God, is more important. Clear your schedule to spend time on a daily basis with your spouse. Date your spouse. Vacate with your spouse. Go to church with your spouse. Read God's Word with your spouse. Pray with your spouse. The two of you have become one flesh!

Time for My Kids

I've heard people say things like, "I can't wait until things settle down so I can spend more time with the kids." Listen, things are actually not going to settle down until the kids *leave.* We need to make time for them *now.* The Bible says, "Children are a gift from the LORD; they are a reward from him. Children born to a young man are like arrows in a warrior's hands. How joyful is the man whose quiver is full of them" (Ps. 127:3–5, NIV). Let's treat them like gifts.

I read an incredibly inspiring story about major league baseball star Ken Griffey, Jr. He was once invited to the Players Choice Awards, where he was to receive the player of the decade award. The Players Choice Awards are broadcast on national television, and are a big deal in the world of baseball. But when Ken Griffey, Jr. found out when the award ceremony was to take place, he declined to attend. He had already made an important commitment on that day—his five-year-old son, Trey, was playing in his first baseball game, and Ken wasn't going to miss it.

Listen, kids are a gift from God, and if you're a parent, your kids need you in their lives. Don't miss out! They need your time and they need your attention. God hardwired them to require your attention. The scary thing is, if you're not giving them the attention they need, they'll find the attention they need in someone else. And unfortunately, you may not get to decide who that person is.

I read a sad and sickening statistic a few years back in USA-Today: Mothers spent nearly twice as much time with their children as fathers did (13.5 hours a week). Even though fathers have nearly tripled their time with children from 2.5 hours in 1965 to 7.3 hours per week in 2011, they're still more likely to feel as if they don't spend as much time as they want with the kids. Think about that for a minute: 13.5 hours per week for moms and 7.3 hours per week for dads. Broken down, that equals 1.9 hours per day for moms, and 1.04 hours per day for dads. That's not enough!

Kids these days spend more time with their electronics than with their parents. Another staggering statistic from USAToday: Kids spend more than 53 hours a week with electronic media—cell phones, iPods, video games, computers, etc.. That's 7.57 hours per day!

Listen, parents: Aside from God, family is first. Your spouse is first and your kids are first. I realize we are busy. But if you're a parent, do whatever it takes. Clear your calendars to spend quality time with your kids each and every day. Again, you'll have to fight for it, but it's worth fighting for. You only have one chance, one shot to raise your kids. Make it count! They're starving for your time and attention. They're starving for your love. Spend time with them. Pray with them and play with them. Read with them and lead them. Talk with them and walk with them. Make memories with them. Be in your child's memories tomorrow, by being in their lives today.

When I was a kid, my mother had a picture hanging on the wall in the living room that displayed the words of Joshua "choose for yourselves this day whom you will serve. . . . But as for me and my household, we will serve the LORD" (Josh. 24:15, NIV). God should not be a piece of your family; he must be the centerpiece. If you're a parent, take the same stance that Joshua took. Make God top priority and first place in your home. Moses said, "Write these commandments that I've given you today on your hearts. Get them inside of you and then get them inside your children. Talk about them wherever you are, sitting at home or walking in the street; talk about them from the time you get up in the morning to when you fall into bed at night. Tie them on your hands and foreheads as a reminder; inscribe them on the doorposts of your homes and on your city gates" (Deut. 6:6-9 MES).

The Most Powerful Two Letters in the Alphabet

The middle two letters of the alphabet can set you free: NO! When you learn to say "no," you learn to manage your time better. When you say "no" to something, you're saying "yes" to *time*. "No" creates margin in your life. "No" creates space in your life. You don't have to say "yes" to everything that comes your way! Just say no!

Ask yourself this question: "What do I need to stop doing in my life right now?" It may not be a bad thing in your life; it just may not be the best thing for your life. As the old saying goes, "If the devil can't make you bad, he'll make you busy." It might even be something you enjoy or that's beneficial, but you simply don't have time for it. What do you need to stop doing?

In her book *A Practical Guide to Prayer*, Dorothy Haskins tells about a noted concert violinist who was asked the secret of her mastery of the instrument. The woman answered the question with two words: "Planned neglect." Then she explained. "There were many things that used to demand my time. When I went to my room after breakfast, I made my bed, straightened my room, dusted, and did whatever seemed necessary. When I finished my work, I turned to my violin practice. That system prevented me from accomplishing what I should have on the violin. So I reversed things. I deliberately planned to neglect everything else until my practice period was complete. And that program of planned neglect is the secret of my success."

Three Keys to Leaving the "BUT . . . I Don't Have Time" Excuse behind You

There you go! Another *but* out of the way! As we close out this chapter, let's revisit three keys that will help you control your calendar, instead of your calendar controlling you, so that you can keep that *but* behind you!

#1—Examine Where Your Time Flies

Yep, time flies—and you're the pilot. So where does your time fly to? It's time for a little self-evaluation! It's time to grab a pen and pad and make a list. Write down all the ways you spend your time each day, and then write down how much time you spend doing them. The key to self-examination is to be real with yourself. Write down where your time flies: work, family, television, cell phone, Instagram, Twitter, or a hobby. Make a bulleted list of where your time goes and how much time it takes. Thorough examination leads to sound information. And as the recovery saying goes, the first step to recovery is admitting you have a problem. Once we can see the "problem," we can move on to step number two.

#2—Prioritize What's Most Important to You

What are the big rocks in your life? Put them in the jar first! As we discussed earlier, God and family first—but what's next? What matters most to you?

It's important to recognize that we can't get everything done, and realize that it's not all worth doing. In the words of Stephen Covey, "The key is not to prioritize what's on your schedule, but to schedule your priorities." The Bible says, "Teach us to number our days and recognize how few they are. Help us to spend them as we should" (Ps. 90:12, LB). Listen: You, and only you, are responsible for how you spend your time. Be responsible. The apostle Paul said, "Live life with a due sense of responsibility, not as those who do not know the meaning and purpose of life but as those who do. Make the best use of your time, despite all the difficulties of these days" (Ephesians, 5:15–16, PH). Start becoming the person you want to be. Choose how you spend your time, rather than letting other priorities choose for you.

#3—Live Passionately, according to Your Priorities

Short and sweet: Make a *list* of the priorities you want to pursue—and then make a *life* of those priorities. Stick to them! No more buts, no more excuses. It's time to shine!

CHAPTER SIX

BUT . . . I'M A FAILURE

The devil might scream that your failure defines you; but God dreams that your failure refines you.

My flesh and my heart may fail, but God is the strength of my heart and my portion forever.

Psalm 73:26, NIV

Fail. Major fail. We've all been there, right? Shattered into a million pieces as we plummet and smash into that dark, lonely pit called rock bottom. Not my favorite place in the world to visit, experiencing the emotions of deep shame, regrets, guilt, embarrassment, sorrow, and remorse. I mean, seriously, how fun is that? But thank God, failure isn't final. Failure is a visitation, not a destination. And thank God that when we fail, God's love and strength *always* prevails.

We've all heard those insanely inspiring stories about people who have hit rock bottom only to climb up, crawl up, claw up, and clamber up to soar to higher heights than they ever soared before. You know the ones: Henry Ford going broke five times before he succeeded; Abraham Lincoln failing in business, having a nervous breakdown, and losing eight elections before he became president; *Star Wars* being rejected by every movie studio in Hollywood until Century Fox finally produced it; and one of my personal favorites, Walt Disney being fired from a newspaper for *lack of ideas*. Um, major fail, newspaper dudes.

Failure is one ugly *but* and a nasty one to hide behind. Failure assaults your character and self-worth relentlessly, and it can keep you discouraged and even debilitated from walking out God's plan and purpose for your life. But the fact is, everyone has failed; and failing should never keep you from sailing. Sure, the devil might scream that your failure defines you; but God dreams that your failure refines you.

The psalmist Asaph said, "My flesh and my heart may fail, but God is the strength of my heart and my portion forever" (Ps. 73:26, NIV). And *your* flesh and heart will fail. That's exactly why God *must* be the strength of your heart and your portion forever. *You* may have failed, but *faith* never fails.

The Bible is full with stories about people who failed. Maybe you've seen this meme floating around cyberspace: "Jacob was a cheater, Peter had a temper, David had an affair, Noah got drunk, Jonah ran away from God, Paul was a murderer, Gideon was insecure, Miriam was a gossiper, Martha was a nervous wreck, Thomas was a doubter, Sarah was impatient, Elijah was depressed, Moses stuttered, Zacchaeus was short, Abraham was old, and Lazarus was dead!" Don't you just love that? The Bible is laced with stories about people who failed themselves, failed other people, and failed God—failures that were so catastrophic, people were left feeling broken, embarrassed, depressed, and completely wrecked. But these stories aren't just about men and women who fell into failure; they're also about how they rose into faith!

Failing into Faith

When most of us hear the words "Peter" and "failure" it's almost natural to immediately think of him denying Christ three times. But there's an incredible story in Luke 5:1–11 where we see Peter (also known as Simon) journey from failure to faith. I'll paraphrase: Peter and his boys had been out fishing all night long, and a failed to catch a single fish. They had to have been tired, disappointed, discouraged, and frustrated. Remember, Peter was a professional fisherman—it was his career. Still, he had failed to catch a single fish all night long. The next morning, as they were washing out their nets, Jesus walked up and decided he wanted to turn Peter's fishing boat into a makeshift stage and podium in order to speak to the crowds. So Peter, his boys, and Jesus hop in the boat and set out off shore a little. Jesus begins preaching to the crowds who were standing on the land. (That's what I'm talking about! Innovation! And a state-of-the-art stage and sound system—and hey, *seaside seating* is better than theater seating.)

After Jesus wraps up his sermon, watch what happens next: "When he finished speaking he said to Simon, 'Put out in deep water and let down the nets for a catch.' Simon answered, 'Master, we've worked hard all night and we haven't caught anything. But because you say so I will let down the nets.' And when they had done so they caught such a large number of fish that their nets began to break" (Luke 5:4–6, NIV).

Seriously, can you imagine? Peter, the fisherman, spent all night fishing and failed to catch anything. Jesus, the carpenter (well, and let's not forget, God in a bod), gets in the boat and tells the boys he wants to go fishing! And I absolutely love Peter's response. Peter's response moved him from failure to faith. "Master, we've worked hard all night and we haven't caught anything. But because you say so I will let down the nets." After having failed to catch a single fish all night long, Peter trusted God and answered Him with a courageous statement of faith, "But because you say so." And they let down their nets and caught so many fish that their nets began to break!

So what was it that took Peter and his boys from failure to faith? It was the same lake, same boat, same nets, same gear, and the same dudes. This difference that moved Peter from failure to faith was *Jesus*. Jesus was now in the boat and was now calling the shots, and *that* is a game changer.

And Jesus wants to do that for you, too. When you let Jesus into your boat and allow him to start calling the shots for your life, just watch how your faith begins to grow. Maybe you're like Peter and you've failed. You're tired, disappointed, discouraged, frustrated. You've worked and put everything you had into a relationship, but it failed. You've worked tirelessly on your business or career, but it failed. You've tried everything in your power to kick that life-controlling habit, and you've failed. Listen: If you want to rise above the fall of failure, you've got to fall forward into the arms of God's grace. Trust God and move from failure to faith. As you forge ahead, make sure Jesus is in your boat and that he's calling the shots for your life. "Trust in the LORD with all your heart and lean not on your own understanding; in all your ways acknowledge him, and he will make your paths straight" (Prov. 3:5–6, NIV).

"Because you say so," God, we will forge ahead from failure to faith.

Focused Faith

Speaking of Peter and faith, one of my favorite stories in the Bible is when Jesus and Peter go for a walk . . . on *water*. I don't know if you've ever tried this, but I have and it's impossible (in fact, it looked like a comedy act!). And as many times as I've heard this story taught, and as many times as I've taught this story, it simply never gets old. But before we jump in, it's important to understand the events and emotional backdrop leading up to this story. I hope you're ready for this, because it's incredible!

Jesus had just heard the devastating news that his beloved cousin, John the Baptist, had been beheaded by King Herod. "When Jesus got the news, he slipped away by boat to an out-of-the-way place by himself. But unsuccessfully—someone saw him and the word got around. Soon a lot of people from the nearby villages walked around the lake to where he was. When he saw them coming, he was overcome with pity and healed their sick" (Matt. 14:13–14, NIV).

Incidentally, "A lot of people from nearby villages" equated to more than five thousand men alone (the men were the only people counted in Bible times)—it could have been 15–25,000 people total, including women and kids—an NBA arena full of people!

This is already amazing. Jesus hears the heartbreaking news about his cousin and hops on a boat in order to get away and spend some alone time—little time to mourn, reflect, and pray. But he gets spotted. And as he's spotted, word spreads like wildfire and the crowds begin to pour in like they're headed to the NBA Finals! And instead of rowing further out to hide so he can get away and mourn, he rows further in and puts his own needs aside to meet the needs of other people. Matthew tells us, "He was overcome with pity and healed their sick." Jesus is heading off to a private prayer session that turns into a healing session that then turns into a dinner session, as he feeds five thousand men and their families. Mind. Blown.

And now, finally, we arrive at the miraculous story about Jesus and Peter walking on water.

After supper was over, Jesus tells his disciples to jump in the boat and head to the other side while he dismisses the crowd (Still amazing, isn't it? He's *still* thinking about the needs of other's and putting other people first.) And now that the people are healed, the people are fed, and his disciples are safely sent off and resting, Jesus finally gets some alone time. He climbs up the mountainside so he can be by himself and pray. I can't imagine the emotions Jesus must have felt at that particular moment. Physically exhausted from meeting the needs of people, and emotionally drained from the devastating news about John. And so, he prays.

Then it's time to catch up with his boys. The only problem is, by this time they're deep out into the water as it's somewhere between 3 to 6 in the morning. Good thing he's *Jesus!*

> Jesus went out to them, walking on the lake. When the
> disciples saw him walking on the lake, they were terrified.
> "It's a ghost," they said, and cried out in fear. But Jesus
> immediately said to them: "Take courage! It is I. Don't
> be afraid." "Lord, if it's you," Peter replied, "tell me to

come to you on the water." "Come," he said. Then Peter got down out of the boat, walked on the water and came toward Jesus. But when he saw the wind, he was afraid and, beginning to sink, cried out, "Lord, save me!" Immediately Jesus reached out his hand and caught him. "You of little faith," he said, "why did you doubt?" And when they climbed into the boat, the wind died down. Then those who were in the boat worshiped him, saying, "Truly you are the Son of God." (Matt. 14:22–33, NIV)

Let's zoom in on this for a second. "Then Peter got down out of the boat, walked on the water and came toward Jesus. But when he saw the wind, he was afraid and, beginning to sink, cried out, 'Lord, save me!'" This is utterly fascinating and on *so* many different levels! When Peter was focused on Jesus and the words of Jesus, he had the faith to get out of the boat and start walking on water; more importantly, he was walking on the very Word of God. His faith had trumped his fear. But when Peter's focus was on the wind, the waves, and the words in his own head, he began to sink.

The same is true for us today. When we walk by faith and upon the Word of God we can walk in the supernatural miracles of God! Second Corinthians 5:7 (ASV) says, "For we walk by faith, not by sight." Instead of constantly focusing on the failures of your past, focus on the faith and Word of God for your future. In the same way that Peter's focus on the wind and waves made him sink, focusing on your failures will make you sink and keep you sunk. If your failures have you sinking today, know what to do before you're sunk. Like Peter, cry out "Lord, save me!" Walk by faith, not by sight. Walk on the Word of God, not on the worries of life. God's Word is full of promises for your life. In fact, one powerful promise you can cling to for your future is this one:

Forget about what's happened; don't keep going over old history. Be alert, be present. I'm about to do something brand-new. It's bursting out! Don't you see it? There it is! I'm making a road through the desert, rivers in the badlands" (Isa. 43:18–19, MES).

I hope you caught that. God is about to do something *brand new* in *you*. Your future starts now. Today is the first day of your brand-new future. Failure is not final, and failure is not fatal!

Keep Fighting

Failure might have knocked you down, but the fact that you're reading these words right now means failure didn't knock you out! You might be on the ropes or you might be at the ninth second on a ten-second knockout count, but you're not knocked out yet. And you're not gonna be! It's time to get the fight back in you. No matter how hard of a blow failure has delivered, never let failure knock you out. Failure doesn't *de*fine you, it only *re*fines you.

I've watched many fights on TV throughout my life. The most memorable, hands down, was Mike Tyson fighting Evander Holyfield in 1997 for the WBC heavyweight championship. Yeah, you know the fight—one of the most bizarre in boxing history. In the first two rounds, Holyfield was wailing on Tyson. As the third round was about to begin, Tyson came out of his corner without his mouthpiece and was ordered back to his corner to insert it. After he had inserted his mouthpiece, he got back into position and the match began, with Tyson launching an all-out attack. But with forty seconds remaining in the round, the tables turned and Holyfield got Tyson in a clinch. Tyson then positioned his head above Holyfield's shoulder and bit Holyfield's right ear! Tyson stepped back to reveal a one-inch piece of cartilage from the top of Holyfield's ear was missing. Tyson then spit it out onto the ring floor.

I'm not exactly sure what was going through Mike's head when he bit Evander (other than Holyfield's fists over and over), but I guess the moral of the story is—or at least what I'm going to make the moral of the story become: Failure delivers hard blows, failure hurts, failure stings, and failure *bites*! (Yes, I had to go there!) Indeed, failure bites, hard. But instead of allowing failure to bite you, you've gotta keep the fight in you!

In this life, we will all experience the tremendous blows in the boxing ring of failure. But no matter how hard of a blow you take, you've gotta keep the fight! Make Second Timothy 4:7 one of your life verses, "I have fought the good fight, I have finished the race, I have kept the faith" (NIV). Keep fighting. Keep the faith.

As you have probably noticed throughout this book, I love the apostle Paul. Either he was an athlete himself, or he was just a complete sports nut, but he regularly used sports analogies throughout his writings. If you're an athlete or a sports nut, the life of Paul would be a great one for you to study! Don't let failure knock you out of God's purpose for your life. Fight the good fight, keep the faith, and finish the race!

Five Keys to Leaving the "BUT . . . I'm a Failure" Excuse behind You

Here are five "Ps" that will lead you to victory, no matter what your fights are, and what your failures have been:

#1—Keep Praying

When failure's got you against ropes, keep praying. Never stop praying. "Pray without ceasing" (1 Thess. 5:17, NASB).

Jesus walked this out. He is our Lord, our Savior, our Master, and our Ruler. And even Jesus, when he was on the ropes, prayed.

In Matthew 26, Jesus was on the ropes big-time. And how did He respond? As you probably already guessed, he went to the Garden of Gethsemane and prayed. This was immediately before he was betrayed and arrested. He knows what lies ahead, he knows he's about to be murdered, and he knows his creation is about to crucify him. He knows he's about to die out of love for man, because of man's hatred toward *him*. He knows he's gonna be beaten, betrayed, mocked, and nailed to a cross. He knows it's not going to be easy.

Jesus didn't fail, but his creation was failing him; so, as he was on the ropes because of other people's failures, he prayed.

Then Jesus came with them to a place called Gethsemane, and said to his disciples, "Sit here while I go over there and pray." And he took with him Peter and the two sons of Zebedee, and began to be grieved and distressed. Then he said to them, "My soul is deeply grieved, to the point of death; remain here and keep watch with me."

And He went a little beyond them, and fell on His face and prayed, saying, "My Father, if it is possible, let this cup pass from me; yet not as I will, but as you will." And He came to the disciples and found them sleeping, and said to Peter, "So, you men could not keep watch with me for one hour? Keep watching and praying that you may not enter into temptation; the spirit is willing, but the flesh is weak."

He went away again a second time and prayed, saying, "My Father, if this cannot pass away unless I drink it, your will be done." Again he came and found them sleeping, for their eyes were heavy. And he left them again, and went away and prayed a third time, saying the same thing once more. Then he came to the disciples and said to them, "Are you still sleeping and resting? Behold, the hour is at hand and the Son of Man is being betrayed into the hands of sinners. Get up, let us be going; behold, the one who betrays me is at hand!" (Matt. 26:36–46, NIV).

When Jesus was on the ropes, he prayed. The Bible says he was grieved and distressed; in fact, it reads: "His soul was deeply grieved to the point of death." And for some of you, this is you. Your failure has you so deeply grieved and distressed, even to the point of death. I encourage you to pray like Jesus prayed. Your life matters.

Your life counts. Your life still has purpose. Failure is not final, and failure is not fatal. Whatever failure has you on the ropes today, pray through it. God is faithful.

#2—Keep Pressing

Paul said, "But one thing I do: Forgetting what is behind and straining toward what is ahead, I press on toward the goal to win the prize for which God has called me heavenward in Christ Jesus" (Phil. 3:13–14, NIV). Forget what's behind and focus on the future. With God in your boat, you can press past your past and toward moving forward. Strain. Don't stop praying and don't stop pressing. When you feel like giving up, keep on keeping on; you just might be at the cusp of your breakthrough!

Maybe you've heard about a woman named Florence Chadwick who attempted to swim from Catalina Island to the California coast in 1952 in an attempt to set a record for covering that twenty-six-mile distance. If you've ever taken the ferry from Catalina to Cali, you know that's a long swim! When she entered the water, a heavy fog had settled itself on the path before her. She swam and swam, but because she was blinded by fog, she became disoriented, discouraged, and eventually gave up. When she finally decided she couldn't go on, her escorts helped her out of the water into a boat. They feared to tell her the reality: she was less than one mile from her goal. Her only reply, after learning how close she actually came, was, "All I could see was hopeless."

Never give up! Keep on keepin' on and keep pressing forward!

#3—Keep Persevering.

There are times in life when all you can do is hold on. Maybe you've heard about a guy named Evans Monsignac. He was buried alive for twenty-seven days in the rubble from the Haiti earthquake. His survival was so remarkable that at times, he said it was easier for him to think that he must be dead. Severely malnourished, dehydrated, deeply traumatized, and with festering wounds, the frail slum-dweller's survival was hailed a miracle when he emerged after an extraordinary twenty-seven days trapped in the ruins. The miracle had doctors completely confounded, as it defied all medical logic. It is believed to be the longest anyone has endured such a trial. Perseverance.

Evans told reporters, "I still don't understand how I'm here, I was resigned to death. But God gave me life. The fact that I'm alive today isn't because of me; it's because of the grace of God. It's a miracle, I can't explain it."

Perseverance is about the ability to endure. And with God in your boat, you can endure and persevere through any storm that life blows your way. Hebrews 12:1-2 (NIV) says, "let us run with perseverance the race marked out for us. Let us fix our eyes on Jesus, the pioneer and perfecter of our faith who for the joy set before him endured the cross, scorning its shame and sat down at the right hand of the throne of God." Paul adds, "We are hard pressed on every side, but not crushed; perplexed, but not in despair; persecuted, but not abandoned; struck down, but not destroyed" (2 Cor. 4:8–9, NIV).

Today, you might be laid out on the ropes of failure, or you might be knocked down and lying flat on your back; but you're not knocked out. Keep fighting. Keep praying. Keep pressing. Keep persevering.

#4—Keep Your Patience

Patience is one of the nine fruits of the Spirit in Galatians 5:22–23 (ESV): "But the fruit of the Spirit is love, joy, peace, patience, kindness, goodness, faithfulness, gentleness and self-control." Patience is a fruit, and if you want to produce good fruit, you have to sow good seeds in good soil. You grow what you sow. You want to be gentle? Sow it! Read Bible verses about being gentle. Pray about being gentle. Hang out with gentle people. Listen to gentle music. Don't watch violent movies. You grow what you sow.

You want patience—sow it. Ask God to help you. Read and memorize Bible verses about patience. Take a deep breath. Remove yourself from the moment. And stay off the freeway!

Again, you grow what you sow. Be patient. God's got you. Keep praying, keep pressing, keep persevering, and keep patient. And finally:

#5—Keep Clinging to God's Promises

No failure, large or small, will ever stop God from loving you. God loves you, with no strings attached. God's love for you isn't based on your performances or successes or failures, it's unconditional. That's true love. And that's God's promise.

> Can anything ever separate us from Christ's love? Does it mean he no longer loves us if we have trouble or calamity, or are persecuted, or hungry, or destitute, or in danger, or threatened with death? No, despite all these things, overwhelming victory is ours through Christ, who loved us. And I am convinced that nothing can ever separate us from God's love. Neither death nor life, neither angels nor demons, neither our fears for today nor our worries about tomorrow—not even the powers of hell can separate us from God's love. No power in the sky above or in the earth below—indeed, nothing in all creation will ever be able to separate us from the love of God that is revealed in Christ Jesus our Lord (Rom. 8:35, 37–39, NLT).

CHAPTER SEVEN

BUT . . . I DON'T HAVE ENOUGH MONEY

I can only imagine all the ministries, businesses and life dreams that were never achieved because they were never conceived due to lack of money.

But my God shall supply all your need according to his riches in glory in Christ Jesus.

Philippians 4:19 KJV

You've got a killer idea for a business, or that burning tug in your heart to launch a new ministry. Perhaps you've also got the money *but*—you know, not enough dollars for the dream. Not enough bread to forge ahead.

Many dreams are often aborted before they ever get started because of the lack of money. And there's no doubt, pursuing a dream without money can be discouraging, if not completely debilitating. I can only imagine all the ministries, businesses, and life dreams that were never achieved because they were never conceived due to lack of money.

What about you? Do you have a dream that you've shelved or even buried because of lack of money? Maybe money has even been the *only* factor. Please allow me to "get my preach on" for a minute: Lack of money should *never* dictate the outcome of your dream. If God drops a dream in your heart, God will drop the means for you to start. God-given dreams will always be fulfilled with God-given means.

93

Philippians 4:19 (KJV) states, "But my God shall supply all your need according to his riches in glory by Christ Jesus." Isn't that awesome? Read that out loud and let that baby resonate deep down in your soul: "But my God shall supply all your need according to his riches in glory by Christ Jesus." And let me tell you something: God is wealthy! God created everything and God owns everything. It's all his. David said, "The earth is the Lord's, and everything in it" (Ps. 24:1a, NIV). Not only is God rich in supply with everything you need, but God knows exactly what you need, when you need it, and how you need it. And of course God's supplies aren't just limited to money, but also toward the countless other needs we all have as well: physical, emotional, and spiritual. God is our supplier. God is our provider.

God Provides

When I first experienced God's Philippians 4:19 provision for my life, I was an eighteen-year-old boy enrolling in Bible school. I had just surrendered my life to Jesus a few months prior, and I was passionate and eager to become a student of God's Word. The problem was, I didn't have any money. Even though I knew this was a God-given dream for my life, I remember questioning whether or not I should even attempt to enroll because of my lack of funds.

Through more prayer and confirmation, I took the leap of faith to enroll in school. Once I did, I experienced one of most memorable and life-changing moments of my life. I was visiting with my Great-Grandma Lee at her house one day as I did quite frequently. Grandma was a woman of God, a woman of faith, and a champion for Christ. She was a prayer warrior. She was also ecstatic that I had just given my life to Christ. In fact, Grandma Lee was one of the many special people in my life who prayed me out of hell and prayed the hell out of me! We all need people like Grandma in our lives.

But Grandma also lived a very hard life. She was a blue-collar, hard-working woman who waited tables most of her life in order to make ends meet. She was a widow living off a fixed Social Security income, which equated to approximately $500 per month. And all of these details are what made this particular day even more special. I'll never forget sitting across from her inside her humble little living room as she said to me, "So Travis, I hear you're going to Bible school?"

"Yes, Grandma, I am!" I said.

What she said next was a defining moment for the foundation of faith in my life: "Well, I want you to know that I am extremely proud of you grandson. I also want you to know that for the past thirty years, I have supported Billy Graham Ministries by sending him $25 per month. But I've decided while you're in Bible school, I am going to redirect my $25 per month to my special grandson, Travis Hearn."

Tears filled my eyes. Did she really just say that? Now don't get me wrong, I realized $25 dollars per month wouldn't even buy enough ramen for a month; but that wasn't the point. The point was worth more than the amount of money involved. The point was that I was watching the beginning stages of God providing the means for my dream right before my very eyes. The point was that I was watching and witnessing the incredible sacrifice and love of my great-grandmother. And hey, let's not forget the third point: I just ousted Billy Graham! Ha!

It was in this moment that I knew beyond a shadow of a doubt that God was going to take care of my every need. I was learning through the test of trust and the school of faith that where God guides, God provides, and where there is vision, there is always provision. It was truly amazing to watch how, over time, God supplied every last penny for my schooling. Grandma Lee has since gone to be with Jesus, and I can't help but think of the pride our Savior must have in such a woman of love, faith, and sacrifice.

Needs, Not Greeds

As much as I am wholeheartedly convinced in God's supernatural provision for each and every one of us, I also feel the responsibility to clarify that God provides for all of our *needs*, and not all our *greeds*. I mean, come on, let's own up to this and call a spade a spade: We are greedy. We live in a greedy world. And our consuming world is consuming our world. Everywhere we go, everywhere we turn, we are smothered by marketing ads that shimmer and shine right in front of our faces with a glittery sparkle that seems to scream, "You need me and you can't live without me!" It's amazing to me how nothing I have ever purchased shimmers and shines when I get it home like it did when it was glimmering in the store.

I don't know about you, but I personally get lured in and sucked in by even the weirdest and wildest infomercials on television. After all, who doesn't need a Potty-Putter, right? Yes, a Potty-Putter. (You guessed it: You practice putting while you're on the potty. I'm not even a golf guy, but that's brilliant!). What we really need an infomercial for is a But-Be-Gone. All of us need to lose that but; that excuse of a feeling that convinces us that we need *everything*, and need it *now*. We buy now and too many times pay for it later, both financially and emotionally. We buy the lie that getting more stuff is what will satisfy our needs. I'm getting off-track here, but again my point is that God provides for all our needs, not our greeds.

In Exodus 16 the Israelites were clearly not enjoying God's journey for their lives nearly as much as I seem to. Then again, I haven't been wandering around the desert (although I do enjoy riding quads around the desert). It's crazy, because the Israelites had just been delivered out of Egyptian slavery a month prior. Although one might assume they'd be ecstatic about their newfound freedom, they were anything *but*. They were complaining about their leaders, Moses and Aaron. They were moaning and groaning about how they wished God would have just killed them back in Egypt and how they were brought to the desert to be starved to death. (By the way, what is it about human nature that makes us feel the need to complain about any and every leader that God places in our lives?) At any rate, the Israelites "weren't feeling it"—their leaders, the desert, their hunger, nothing. It was pretty absurd, too, because these guys had been firsthand witnesses of God's supernatural provision time and time again. Nevertheless, they continued to grumble, bellyache, and worry that God wouldn't provide for them *this time around*. But God knew exactly what they needed, exactly when they needed it, and exactly how they needed it. Take a look at what Exodus 16:11-18 (NLT) says, and notice the use of the word *need*:

> Then the Lord said to Moses, "I have heard the Israelites' complaints. Now tell them, 'In the evening you will have meat to eat, and in the morning you will have all the bread you want. Then you will know that I am the Lord your God.'" That evening vast numbers of quail flew in and covered the camp. And the next morning the area around the camp was wet with dew. When the dew evaporated, a flaky substance as fine as frost blanketed the ground. The Israelites were puzzled when they saw it. "What is it?" they asked each other. They had no idea what it was. And Moses told them, "It is the food the Lord has given you to eat. These are the Lord's instructions: Each household should gather as much as it needs. Pick up two quarts for each person in your tent." So the people of Israel did as they were told. Some gathered a lot, some only a little. But when they measured it out, everyone had just enough. Those who gathered a lot had nothing left over, and those who gathered only a little had enough. Each family had just what it needed.

Spectacular, right? Yay for God! "Each household should gather as much as it needs" and "each family had just what it needed." God will provide for your needs, too.

Guiding Lights

Most of the time, I sincerely enjoy the journey of "figuring out God's plan" for my life. It's quite adventurous. It's like solving an equation, or working on a puzzle. Sure, God's direction and journey for my life would be far more convenient and easier to understand if he'd crack open the skies and speak to me in an audible voice, but that would also take away so many exciting miracles like faith, seeking God, being still and listening to him, ongoing conversations with him, and even confirmations and the fun and different ways he provides them. The fact remains true: God guides.

A couple of years ago, my daughter Kylie and I took a trip with her school to her science camp at Catalina Island. I've gotta say, if you ever get the chance to go, go! This camp was so much fun and thoroughly educational. During the five days of this camp we enjoyed midnight snorkeling, hiking, rock-wall climbing, kayaking, and so much more.

One day, we got to experience something called the blind maze. From the outside, this maze looked like a backyard wood-shed. But on the inside, it was a blacked-out maze. You had to drop to your knees and crawl in through a small hatch door and then scramble forward as you felt your way through the blind maze until you came out the correct door. Inside the maze, you couldn't see a thing. It was completely dark! You'd crawl forward, backward, upward, and downward, and within minutes you were completely turned around and confused. Kylie went through this maze before I did and I could hear her giggle and scream as she felt her way through the maze with her friends. But then, it was my turn. Ugh. I've never considered myself claustrophobic, but this felt like I was in a blacked-out elevator with no ventilation, with walls that were closing in on me! As I crawled around, hitting all the dead ends, I started to panic. Yes, a full-grown man inside a kids' science camp maze and I was under complete distress. As I forged ahead, I went up and down and all around, hitting wall after wall. But finally, I spotted a glimmer of light. As I quickly scaled across the floor, I pushed open the door to breathe in fresh air and see the sunlight.

The blind maze reminds me of our walk and journey with God. Without God's guiding light, we are simply blind, stressed-out people who end up turned around and confused by the ups and downs in the maze of life. But with God, we have a guiding light to lead us through life's journey.

The Good Book Guide Book

One of the main guiding lights for our lives is the guidebook God wrote for our lives, the Holy Bible. The Bible is the roadmap for our lives. It's the GPS—God's Positioning System—for our lives. Psalm 119:105 (ESV) says, "Your word is a lamp to my feet and a light to my path." God's Word will guide us into safety, away from danger, through the storms of life, and step by step as we pursue his purpose for our lives.

If you're looking for guidance and direction for your life, you must look to the Holy Bible—not just reading it, but devouring it. Make time for it. Memorize it. Meditate on it. And as you engage with God's Word, get ready, because the word of God will inspect you, dissect you, correct you, protect you, and of course, direct you. The Bible is God's Word for our lives!

I love the way Paul puts it in 2 Timothy. This letter contains some of Paul's final words. He was imprisoned in Rome, realizing that his life was about to come to an end, and in this letter he seems to state the things that mattered most to him. He told Timothy and those he was pastoring, "All Scripture is God-breathed and is useful for teaching, rebuking, correcting and training in righteousness, so that the servant of God may be thoroughly equipped for every good work" (2 Timothy 3:16–17, NIV). What a great way to summarize the purpose and the power of the Word of God!

If your desire is to be trained and equipped for God's journey for your life, you must understand the importance of God's Word as the guide for your life. No one should ever make a decision, major or minor, without first referring to the Word of God. The Good Book is our guidebook; it's the manual from Immanuel.

What decisions are you about to make in life? Whether you're thinking about launching a business, making a career move, beginning a family, or anything else, don't you dare make move without referring to God's guidebook!

The Holy Spirit

The other major guiding light for our lives is the Holy Spirit. In the original Greek, "Holy Spirit" means "the one called alongside to help." Isn't that cool? And that's exactly what the Holy Spirit does for us. God's Spirit is one of the three members of the Godhead in the Holy Trinity: God the Father, Jesus the Son, and The Holy Spirit. Jesus told us that he was giving us the Holy Spirit as our advocate (helper) who would never leave us.

> And I will ask the Father, and he will give you another Advocate, who will never leave you. He is the Holy Spirit, who leads into all truth. The world cannot receive him, because it isn't looking for him and doesn't recognize him. But you know him, because he lives with you now and later will be in you. No, I will not abandon you as orphans—I will come to you" (John 14:16–19, NLT).

If you're a Christian, the Holy Spirit dwells within you. Indeed, the Bible says: "Do you not know that you are a temple of God and that the Spirit of God dwells in you?" And, "do you not know that your body is a temple of the Holy Spirit who is in you, whom you have from God, and that you are not your own?" (1 Cor. 3:16; 6:19, NIV).

There are countless functions of the Holy Spirit in our lives. To name a few: The Holy Spirit convicts us, convinces us, comforts us, counsels us, teaches us, helps us to stop sinning, gives us discernment, gives us peace, and even helps us to pray and preach and teach. But one of the major functions of the Holy Spirit that we will zoom in on is guidance. God's Spirit guides us.

In the Bible, we read many times when the Holy Spirit guided people. Jesus was led by the Spirit into the wilderness (Matthew 4). Philip was led by the Spirit to the Eunuch (Acts 8). Peter was led by the Spirit to the house of Cornelius (Acts 10). Paul was led by the Holy Spirit during his three missionary journeys throughout the book of Acts. God's Spirit guided them, and he will guide us as well.

Finance Problems or Faith Problems

Again, God guides; and where God guides, he also provides. You have to trust him to pave the way. Trust him to turn the water into wine. Trust him to drop the manna from the sky. Trust him to provide the loaves and the fishes. "Trust in the Lord with all your heart, and lean not on your own understanding: in all your ways acknowledge Him, and He shall direct your paths" (Prov. 3:5–6, NIV). When God gives you the dream, he always gives you the means. There is never a money problem, only a mental problem. There's never a finance problem, only a faith problem.

The obstacle is never about the supply of finances, but about the supply of faith. How high is your faith supply? God loves to make a way out of "no way." He loves to transcend every dead end. He loves to turn limitation into multiplication! After all, it was Jesus himself who said, "With man this is impossible, but with God all things are possible" (Matt. 19:26, NIV). God's got your back. He works in mysterious ways, guides in mysterious ways, and provides in mysterious ways.

God's provision reminds me of a story I told in my first book, *Game Changer*. The story is about a hunter who walked through the African jungle and found a huge dead warthog with a pygmy standing beside it. Amazed, he asked: "Did you kill that warthog?"

The pygmy said, "Yes."

The hunter asked, "How could such a little guy like you kill a huge beast like that?"

"I killed it with my club," the pygmy answered.

The astonished hunter asked, "How big is your club?"

The pygmy replied, "There's about sixty of us."

And that's exactly the kind of backing God has for you. No matter how little your resources might seem, God's the one who provides for the dream. Shoot, even the mighty dollar screams, "In God We Trust." So go ahead, take that audacious step of faith. Walk by faith, not by sight. Trust God with your dream, and trust God with your means.

Five Keys to Leaving the "BUT . . . I Don't Have Enough Money" Excuse behind You

#1—Commit Your Dream to God

"Commit to the LORD whatever you do, and he will establish your plans" (Prov. 16:3, NIV). The most important step in planning and dreaming is to dedicate those plans and dreams to God. Whether it's your business, relationship or marriage, finances, or simply your life, hand it over to God. All of it. And hold nothing back. You'll have to fully let go before he can fully take hold.

Give God everything you've got and watch him multiply your life and your resources. Just like the boy in John 6 who gave Jesus the two small fish and the five small barley loaves of bread, when you give everything you've got to Jesus, that's when he can fully bless it and multiply it.

#2—Trust That God Will Provide

Remember, God created everything and God owns everything. Commit your dream to God and trust that he will provide. God can see the future; he can see next week, next year, fifty years from now. Psalm 81 reminds us that God is our provider. Even after God miraculously delivered the Israelites out of slavery from Egypt, they constantly lived with worry and fear that God would now not provide. But he did, and he still does. "I, the LORD, am your God, who brought you up from the land of Egypt; open your mouth wide and I will fill it" (Ps. 81:10, NIV).

Open your mouth and trust God to fill the needs for your dream. God shall supply all your needs, according to his riches and glory (Phil. 4:19).

#3—Pray

Praying about your dream goes hand-in-hand with committing your dream to God. Pray that God will pour out his favor onto your life to fulfill your God-sized dream. Pray that God supernaturally sends the resources. Pray for connections, relationships, and a network that you could have never had on your own. Pray that God will open doors that no man can open, and pray that God will close any door you shouldn't walk through.

And to take it one step further: Grab a friend to pray with you about it. Confide your dream in a trusted God-fearing friend who has your best interests in mind—someone who will keep your dreams in confidence and who will earnestly pray for you and with you. Jesus said, "When two of you get together on anything at all on earth and make a prayer of it, my Father in heaven goes into action. And when two or three of you are together because of me, you can be sure that I'll be there" (Matt. 18:20, MES).

#4—Walk by Faith, Not by Sight

Focus with your mind's eye and not your physical eyes. It's time to "walk by faith, not by sight" (2 Cor. 5:7, NKJV). When launching out into any dream or plan, there's a tall stairway of faith steps that you'll have to take, and you'll have to take them one step at a time.

As your foot hits the top step of the sky-high stairway and you realize you haven't reached your goal yet, keep in mind that there's another step above the one you're standing on, but that you may not be able to see it yet. You're going to have to step out in faith before the step appears. As you put your complete trust in God, and put your faith into action, you'll be able to watch God part the Red Seas in your life.

#5—Acknowledge God as Your Provider

Always remember, and never forget, that God provides. As you achieve your dreams, remember that we are nothing without Christ. God is our provider. God has given you the skill set and the mindset, so never forget the onset. He created you and he provides for you every step of the way.

When Abraham was asked and tested by God to sacrifice his son, Isaac, he obediently walked up that mountain with complete faith and trust, believing that God knew best. And as Abraham passed the test of trust with flying colors, God provided a different sacrifice: a ram. I love what Abraham does next:

> Abraham looked up and there in a thicket he saw a ram caught by its horns. He went over and took the ram and sacrificed it as a burnt offering instead of his son. So Abraham called that place The Lord Will Provide. And to this day it is said, "On the mountain of the Lord it will be provided" (Gen. 22:13–14, NIV).

Never forget: It's God who provides.

CHAPTER EIGHT

BUT...I'M NOT EXPERIENCED OR EDUCATED

God isn't looking for the most educated, he's looking for the most dedicated.

Take a good look, friends, at who you were when you got called into this life. I don't see many of "the brightest and the best" among you, not many influential, not many from high-society families. Isn't it obvious that God deliberately chose men and women that the culture overlooks and exploits and abuses, chose these "nobodies" to expose the hollow pretensions of the "some-bodies"? That makes it quite clear that none of you can get by with blowing your own horn before God. Everything that we have—right thinking and right living, a clean slate and a fresh start—comes from God by way of Jesus Christ. That's why we have the saying, "If you're going to blow a horn, blow a trumpet for God."

1 Corinthians 1:27–31, MES

I heard a story about two fishermen who went on a fishing trip. They rented all their gear: the reels, the rods, the wading suits, the rowboat, the SUV, and even a cabin in the woods. They had racked up a monster bill before they'd even neared the edge of the water. The first day they went fishing, they didn't catch a single fish! The second and third days produced the same results, nada. Finally, on the fourth day, one of the fishermen caught a fish. As they were driving home they were extremely disappointed about their fishing trip. One guy turned to the other and said, "Do you realize that this one lousy fish we caught cost us about two grand?"

The other guy said, "Wow! It's a good thing we didn't catch any more!"

Nobodies into Somebodies

This story makes me think about Peter in Matthew 4. Peter had no idea what was ahead. He had no clue that the fishing trip he was about to go on was going to cost him his life. I mean, think of it, Peter was a fisherman and he went on fishing trips every single day of his life. It's what he did. But this wasn't going to be just another fishing trip—this was a fishing trip that was going to cost him his entire life! He was about to lay down his nets and take up his cross, and God was about to take him from being a person in a boat to a powerhouse in the Bible.

Cool, right? Why would God do that, anyway? Why would God have any interest in using a local fisherman to become a global world-changing fisher of men? Because that's exactly what God does—over and over again. He uses ordinary people to do extraordinary acts for God. He uses the normal to do the abnormal. God turns fishermen into fishers of men. He turns persecutors into preachers. God turns falling stars into superstars! God specializes in turning the nobodies into somebodies. That's just what he does! He can't help himself!

God's not looking for the most educated; he's looking for the most dedicated. He puts his stamp of approval, favor, and anointing upon those who say, "Yes, Lord!" I've seen God do it time and time again. There's nothing more exciting and energizing than when God calls an ordinary person who wasn't on anybody else's radar screen to do the extraordinary—when he taps the shoulders of the nobodies of the world whom the rest of the world overlooked and says, "I pick you. I need you. I want you on *my* team."

I'm convinced that one of the ways God displays his sovereignty is by transforming the least likely into what turns out to be the most obvious. Paul said it like this:

> Take a good look, friends, at who you were when you got called into this life. I don't see many of "the brightest and the best" among you, not many influential, not many from high-society families. Isn't it obvious that God deliberately chose men and women that the culture overlooks and exploits and abuses, chose these "nobodies" to expose the hollow pretensions of the "somebodies"? That makes it quite clear that none of you can get by with blowing your own horn before God. Everything that we have—right thinking and right living, a clean slate and a fresh start—comes from God by way of Jesus Christ. That's why we have the saying, "If you're going to blow a horn, blow a trumpet for God" (1 Cor. 1:27–31, MES).

Tapped, But Trapped

Awesome, right? God deliberately chooses the men and women that culture overlooks and turns the nobodies into somebodies! He's deliberate. He's purposeful. He chooses men and women that culture overlooks to become powerhouses for his kingdom.

But there's a problem, and there always has been a problem—and that problem is the human heart. It's the insecurities and the selfishness of people as we battle and war against the qualifying call of God. I wonder how many times throughout history, God has tapped the shoulders of people who never allowed God to use them. *I wonder how many times God has qualified the called, but those who were called chose to remain unqualified.* He spoke to them, whispered to their hearts, confirmed his calling, and yet, they chose to remain unqualified. They were tapped on, but they tapped out.

How many people have stayed on the sidelines because of doubts, fears, or even because of those tantalizing things of this world like "the lust of the flesh, the lust of the eyes, and the pride of life" (1 John 2:16. KJV)? Sadly, too many times, the things of this world lure us in, trap us, and keep from becoming who God created us to be.

I heard a fascinating story about a tactic African hunters use to trap baboons. The hunter knows that baboons are highly inquisitive. So the trapper will dig a small tunnel hole into a berm or embankment, with a larger hole at the back end. He then places wild melon seeds in the bigger part of the hole in the back end of the berm and then he simply walks away and waits. Burning with curiosity about what's in the hole, the baboon stares at it. It eats at him and eventually, he just can't take it anymore. He walks over the hole, looks inside, sticks his arm deep into the back end, and grabs a fistful of melon seeds. The baboon is thrilled to be holding these mouthwatering melon seeds in his hands! However, now that he has his fist clenched, his hand is too big to come out of the hole. He's trapped! If only he'd simply let go of those seeds, he could get his arm out. The problem is, he won't. He absolutely has to have those melon seeds!

That's one of the very same tactics the devil traps you and I in, keeping us from becoming all that God created us to be. He lures us and baits us with the enticing things of this world like pride, possessions, prestige, and power. He also lures us and baits us with doubts, fears, or insecurities and we're too scared or insecure or selfish to let them go. Therefore, we are trapped; we become indefensible and vulnerable to the trapper's agenda for our lives.

But God is looking for the usable—those who are undistracted and dedicated. He's looking for those who will let go, open their hands, and raise them high to the sky and boldly declare, "God, I'm yours!" God's looking for those who fling off the world and cling to the Word. He is searching for those who will let go of their own cravings, lusts, and desires, and grab hold of the hands of their Savior.

Don't get me wrong; I'm a strong believer in education and experience. Both will undoubtedly make every one of us more effective in our tireless work for Jesus. In fact, I strongly recommend you never stop educating yourself. Be a life-learner. But also please understand, there are many people who are highly educated and experienced who are never used by God, because being usable isn't about how educated you are, it's about how dedicated you are.

God's Goggles

I have learned through the years that lack of education and experience can simply become another excuse that we make—a huge *but* that gets in our way. But God looks at our lives and résumés through a different set of lenses than society does. I call these lenses "God's Goggles." God looks for the usable. God *uses* the usable.

In the Bible, God saw the beauty, and perhaps the humor, in using a donkey to speak to Balaam. Jesus saw something in his closest disciples, two sets of brothers who were merely fishermen, Peter and Andrew and James and John. God saw something in David when he chose this underaged, undertrained, under-experienced and under-armed shepherd boy, to slay the soldier of all soldiers, Goliath. Oh, and how about this one: God saw a diamond in the rough when he chose Mary to be the mother of God's one and only Son. God didn't choose a wealthy queen from a high-class city who was educated or who had any experience as a mother. He chose Mary, an unmarried, lower-middle-class woman who lived in one of the most disliked cities in Israel, Nazareth. God loves to defy the odds so that there's no way to deny that it *is* God who's doing it.

God sees you the same way; through his goggles. God qualifies the called. He uses the usable. I am a classic example of this. I'm a small-town boy from a broken family with a family line of addicts and prisoners. My family is flawed. I am flawed. There's not a day in my life when I don't feel like a little leaguer playing in a major league baseball game. Unqualified. Under-experienced. Under-every-thinged. (Yes, I made that word up.) I write and preach sermons for a church full of people, many of whom are more intelligent, more educated, make more money, and even know more Bible than I do. At the same time, I've led Bible studies with pro athletes sitting across from me like Kevin Durant, Russell Westbrook, Dwight Howard, Stephen Curry, Clay Thompson, Chris Paul and hundreds more—people who are looking for answers, support, leadership, and guidance. Talk about feeling insecure, inadequate, and inferior!

And here's another glimpse of God's humor for you coupled with his uncanny ability to use our inability: I've even led worship while playing the guitar and singing songs to Jesus in a locker room full of major league baseball players, with Garth Brooks sitting next to me! Yes, *the* Garth Brooks sitting right by my side, smiling, singing, clapping, and praising God! You see, God uses the usable.

People have asked me throughout the years, "Travis, how did you get that Phoenix Suns gig?" (You'd be shocked how many people have called the Phoenix Suns ministry a "gig."). I'm convinced the answer has everything to do with the fact that God uses the usable and the dedicated. I didn't interview for it. I didn't put a resumé together for it. God simply opened a door for an under-experienced twenty-five-year-old who was usable.

Rationalize or Rational Lies

Life is crazy! I'll never forget when I was seventeen years old sitting in a church service when God clearly spoke to my heart about going on a missions trip to Mazatlan, Mexico. I was a brand-new Christian, just a few months old, and I was bursting with excitement and expectation to be used by God. For the first time in my life, I had heard God's voice speak to me through an overwhelming impression. I signed up for the trip, raised enough money to go, and attended all the trainings that led up to the mission. I was ready!

That's when one of the hardest tests of my life arrived in my mailbox. There was a large envelope addressed to me from the Arizona Interscholastic Association. The AIA is the organization that governs all high school sports for the state of Arizona. As I opened the envelope, I soon realized that it was a congratulatory package and an invitation to participate and play in the Arizona All-Star Basketball Game and Events. I couldn't believe it! I'd made it! I made the team! I was so excited! Playing in this game was a childhood dream of mine! You have to understand, basketball was my life. (By the way, did you know basketball is God's favorite sport? After all, Jesus *did* perfect the cross-over. . . and, *his* hang time will forever be the most famous logo in the history of eternity; step aside, MJ. OK, I digress.)

As I continued to read through the material, my heart sank, as I quickly realized that the AIA game and events were the *exact* same dates as my missions trip to Mazatlan. Literally, same start date, same finish date. Ugh!

I truly believe the decision I was about to make is what shaped the rest of my life. This was a test, on so many different levels. This was a test about my priorities. This was a test of selfishness or selflessness. This was a test about fulfilling my dream or God's dream. This was a test about my face shining in the spotlight or my faith shining around God's light. This was a test about obedience. This was a test about listening to the still, small voice of *God*—or listening to the overwhelming shouts of self and man. This was a test about compromises, justifications, and rationalizations.

Sure, I could have rationalized. We all can, and we all do. But to rationalize is to make up rational lies. And ultimately, this was a test about which God I really served, Jesus or Travis. I'm also convinced that this very decision would allow me to walk in God's qualifying call, or would allow me to remain unqualified for his call.

I had countless friends, parents, teachers, administrators—shoot, even a godly NFL player—tell me I was crazy, that I was making a bad decision. They told me things like, "Travis, there are countless other missions trips you could go on fifty-one other weeks of the year." And there were. But that wasn't the point. At least, it wasn't *God's* point.

I made my decision. I picked up the phone and dialed the AIA myself. I was scared. I told them that I was incredibly honored, but that I would not be able to attend because I had just become a Christian and God called me to go on a missions trip to Mazatlan that happened to be the exact same timeframe. The gentleman on the phone was kind, but he also expressed his concerns and disagreements. Although he commended me for my faith, he also laid out all the reasons he thought I was making a bad decision. And at the end of our conversation he told me, "Well, Travis, one good thing that will come out of this for sure is that we will call an honorable mention up and this will make his year!" (Glad I could help.)

As I look back twenty-two years later, I still remember this entire life-lesson like it was yesterday. In fact, it's funny, in a not-so-funny way, because this same lesson presents itself to me over and again, disguised in different forms. The lesson is simply: Whom do you serve, God or Travis?

But I can tell you this: Going to Mazatlan was one of the best decisions I've ever made in my life. As I was in Mazatlan, I had the privilege of personally leading a man to Jesus! I remember it was the same night, and at the same time the All-Star game was being played back in Arizona. As my mind flashed back to what might be happening in the game at that moment, tears were streaming down this gentleman's face as we prayed together and he accepted Jesus into his life. And it was in that moment that I discovered there is nothing greater in the world to live for than Jesus Christ and watching people come to know him as their Lord and Savior just like I did. And who knows, maybe the faith, surrender, sacrifice, and obedience involved with the decision I made is the very reason why one day God would open a door for me to serve as the team pastor for the Phoenix Suns and influence the influencers with the peace, love, and joy of Jesus Christ.

Slay It

I'm certain that every person who follows Christ will have their own story of surrender and sacrifice. In fact, Jesus said, "Whoever wants to be my disciple must deny themselves and take up their cross daily and follow me" (Luke 9:23, NIV). And my story of testing doesn't hold a candle Abraham's story of testing:

> Some time later God tested Abraham. He said to him, "Abraham!" "Here I am," he replied. Then God said, "Take your son, your only son, whom you love—Isaac —and go to the region of Moriah. Sacrifice him there as a burnt offering on a mountain I will show you." Early the next morning Abraham got up and loaded his donkey. He took with him two of his servants and his son Isaac. When he had cut enough wood for the burnt offering, he set out for the place God had told him about. On the third day Abraham looked up and saw the place in the distance. He said to his servants, "Stay here with the donkey while I and the boy go over there. We will worship and then we will come back to you. Abraham took the wood for the burnt offering and placed it on his son Isaac, and he himself carried the fire and the knife. As the two of them went on together, Isaac spoke up and said to his father Abraham, "Father?" "Yes, my son?" Abraham replied. "The fire and wood are here," Isaac said, "but where is the lamb for the burnt offering?" Abraham answered, "God himself will provide the lamb for the burnt offering, my son." And the two of them went on together. When they reached the place God had told him about, Abraham built an altar there and arranged the wood on it. He bound his son Isaac and laid him on the altar, on top of the wood. Then he reached out his hand and took the knife to slay his son. But the angel of the Lord called out to him from heaven,

"Abraham! Abraham!" "Here I am," he replied. "Do not lay a hand on the boy," he said. "Do not do anything to him. Now I know that you fear God, because you have not withheld from me your son, your only son." Abraham looked up and there in a thicket he saw a ram caught by its horns. He went over and took the ram and sacrificed it as a burnt offering instead of his son. So Abraham called that place The Lord Will Provide. And to this day it is said, "On the mountain of the Lord it will be provided" (Gen. 22:1–14, NIV).

No matter how many times I read this story, it always seems to leave me a little dumbfounded. God asked Abraham to sacrifice his one and only son (sound familiar?). And this was not *just* his one and only son—this was the one and only son he'd been waiting for his whole life! I like how pastor and author Mark Batterson articulated this in his book *All In*, "The harder you have to work for something, the harder it is to give it up. And the longer you have to wait for it, the tougher it is to give it back. That's why Abraham's all-in moment was so amazing. Isaac was the lifelong dream of a barren woman named Sarah and an impotent man named Abraham." And now, God put a test before Abraham and asked him to sacrifice his one and only miracle son on the altar. Remarkably enough, it's also a test Abraham passed with flying colors!

What is *your* Isaac? We all have one. What's yours? What is that one thing in your life you possess that just might be possessing you? What are the wild melon seeds inside the palms of your hands you're selfishly refusing to let go of? Maybe it's fears or failures; maybe it's pride or prestige; maybe it's insecurities or inferiorities; or maybe it's even possessions or people. Whatever your Isaac may be, it's not only time to lay it down, it's time to sacrifice it. Slay it. Like Peter did, lay down your nets, take up your cross and be usable! God wants to qualify you. God's not looking at your education; he's looking at your dedication. Are you willing to lay it all down so he can use you all up?

Four Keys to Leaving the "BUT . . . I'm Not Experienced or Educated" Excuses behind You

#1—Be Dedicated

Remember, God's not looking for the most educated; he's looking for the most dedicated. Are you dedicated? Remember what Jesus said to his disciples when he was looking for the usable, "Whoever wants to be my disciple must deny themselves and take up their cross and follow me. For whoever wants to save their life will lose it, but whoever loses their life for me will find it. What good will it be for someone to gain the whole world, yet forfeit their soul? Or what can anyone give in exchange for their soul?" (Matt. 16:24–26, NIV). Lose your life for Jesus; he lost his life for yours!

#2—Be Stripped

Open up your hands and throw down those melon seeds! The writer of Hebrews said, "let us strip off every weight that slows us down, especially the sin that so easily trips us up. And let us run with endurance the race God has set before us" (Heb. 12:1, NLT). Lay down your Isaac. Lay down that one thing, or two things, or twenty things in your life you possess that just might be possessing you—those things that have the ability to keep you from walking out God's qualifying call for your life. Throw them down. Lay down your nets and take up your cross.

#3—Be Focused

Don't get slowed down, weighted down, or baited down by any distractions or "wild melon seeds" that the devil tries to lure you with. Stay focused. Jesus said, "No one who puts a hand to the plow and looks back is fit for service in the kingdom of God" (Luke 9:62,

NIV). Don't look to the left or to the right, and definitely don't look back. Keep your eyes focused on our prized Savior and press forward.

#4—Be Filled

Be filled and overflowing with God's Holy Spirit. Spend time with Jesus each and every day in prayer and in his Holy Word. The more you're influenced by Jesus, the more you'll influence for Jesus. God can give you more wisdom and knowledge than any book or school could ever attempt. I love what Acts says about Peter and John: "When they saw the courage of Peter and John and realized that they were unschooled, ordinary men, they were astonished and they took note that these men had been with Jesus. . . . they could not stand up against the wisdom the Spirit gave him as he spoke" (Acts 4:13; 6:10, NIV). Go ahead, astonish some people! Spend time with Jesus.

CHAPTER NINE

BUT...I'M TOO TIRED

Sometimes in life, I feel like I'm running downhill. There's a fine line between running faster than I've ever run, and falling harder than I've ever fallen.

Come to me, all you who are weary and burdened, and I will give you rest. Take my yoke upon you and learn from me, for I am gentle and humble in heart, and you will find rest for your souls. For my yoke is easy and my burden is light.

Matthew 11:28–30, NIV

The bills are washed, the laundry is paid, the clothes are in the oven, and the last load of dinner is in the dryer. But you did it! If you're anything like me, you already want to take a nap, tomorrow.

Your tired *but* has kept you from accomplishing many goals in life, or it has helped you accomplish the wrong goals in life. You're tired. You're fatigued. You're not lazy; you're just exhausted and completely wiped out. You need to clean the house or the car or the garage, but you're too tired. You need to make that phone call or send that email, but your energy level isn't seeing eye-to-eye with you. I feel you. Sometimes in life, I feel like I'm running downhill and there's a fine line between running faster than I've ever run, and falling harder than I've ever fallen. Maybe you can relate.

Life can just be flat overwhelming! Too much to do and too little time to do it. The incessant pressures, stress, and busyness of today's fast-paced, high-demand lifestyle leave you completely wiped out! Maybe you feel like Job when he said, "I have no peace! I have no quiet! I have no rest! And trouble keeps coming!" (Job 3:26, GWT). According to The National Institutes of Health, approximately one in every five Americans claims to have fatigue that is severe enough to interfere with normal daily life. So how do you press through when you're pressed down?

I want to give you the biblical prescription for tapping into God's power and energy, so that you can eliminate fatigue from being that big debilitating *but* in your life.

Rest

One day, as I pulled up to a stop light, there was a homeless man standing on the street corner holding a piece of cardboard that read, "Hanging in there like a loose tooth." I got a little chuckle out of it, and thought to myself, "You and everybody else, brother!" Many people are so beat up, beat down, and pulled back and forth that they are simply hanging in there like a loose tooth. But God doesn't want us to simply hang in there; he wants us to hang on to him.

One of the biblical remedies for staying refreshed is proper rest. In other words, in order to keep going, you need to keep stopping. It's important to understand that rest is spiritual and rest is biblical. Getting proper rest is mandatory if we want to remain spiritually, emotionally, and physically healthy.

I do realize that some people view resting as an attribute of laziness. And there seems to be some sort of societal bragging right to having little rest or even no rest at all. I've heard people say things like, "I only need four hours of sleep every night," or "I never take naps, I don't need them," or, "I work eighty-to-ninety-hour weeks." (Yeah, well, good for them, and maybe that would explain why they're so danged irritable and grouchy!)

To many people, the need for rest seems to equate to being soft or weak. But I'd like to reorient their thinking toward the fact that even God rested. Rest is biblical and rest is a requirement from

God. So, let that idea set your weak and weary mind free! Rest is not only a good thing, but rest is a God thing! King Solomon put it like this: "Only someone too stupid to find his way home would wear himself out with work" (Eccl. 10:15, GNT). Ouch! So don't be stupid. Get some rest!

Obviously, lack of rest has major implications on our lives. Lack of rest causes accidents, dumbs you down, causes health problems, causes depression, ages your skin, makes you forgetful, makes you gain weight, and impairs your judgment. I'd like to add to this list that lack of rest makes you irritable, diminishes your patience, and demotivates you.

But the good news is that God created rest, God created you to rest and God rested himself! In fact, when God rested on that day, the Bible goes as far as to say that day was blessed! Check it out:

> By the seventh day God had finished the work he had been doing; so on the seventh day he rested from all his work. And God blessed the seventh day and made it holy, because on it he rested from all the work of creating that he had done (Gen. 2:2–3, NIV).

Imagine that! God—rested? Talk about a power nap! "God blessed the seventh day and made it holy." Now that's what I'm talking about! Rest that is blessed!

Rest is such an important matter to God that he put it in the Ten Commandments, along with not murdering, not stealing, and not committing adultery. And not only did he mention it, but he also modeled it—"so on the seventh day he rested from all his work." Listen, if God needs to rest from his work, how much *more* rest do you and I need from our work? Let's look at what he says in Exodus 20:8-11 (NIV):

> Remember the Sabbath day by keeping it holy. Six days you shall labor and do all your work, but the seventh day

is a sabbath to the Lord your God. On it you shall not do any work, neither you, nor your son or daughter, nor your male or female servant, nor your animals, nor any foreigner residing in your towns. For in six days the Lord made the heavens and the earth, the sea, and all that is in them, but he rested on the seventh day. Therefore the Lord blessed the Sabbath day and made it holy.

God not only mentioned it, he also modeled it. God rested and he created you for rest. Rest is not a recommendation; it's a biblical requirement. In addition to a spiritual law, being well rested not only keeps you motivated, but keeps you healthy. In fact, studies have shown that taking regular mental breaks can increase creativity, productivity, memory capability, and focus. If you find yourself too tired and exhausted to face your days, you might just need to take a nap!

Relaxation

"Take a chill pill!" "Relax already, would ya'?" Most of the time, those statements are used in a negative context, but I'll use them in a positive context. Sincerely, I mean it, with all my heart, relax already, would ya'? Relaxing goes hand in hand with resting, although it shares its differences. Relaxing doesn't necessarily involve sleeping but unwinding, kicking back, and decompressing.

Yeah, yeah, I get it, you probably don't even have the time to relax, do ya'? I've got news for you: If this is the case, you need to *make* the time because you need the rest. The moment you know you need down time is the moment you don't have enough time for down time. As I mentioned earlier, you have time for what you have time for. And you'd be amazed at how much extra time you'd have for down time if you'd make the *most* of your time. It may just be that you need to create a little margin in your life. Cut some things out that don't matter, or that don't matter as much.

Remember, prioritize! Rest and relaxation are big rocks. Go to bed earlier. Don't watch that late-night TV show. Don't drink that triple-shot latte at 10 at night! Create a disciplined rest schedule that will help you succeed in getting the proper rest and relaxation that your body needs.

Slow Down

Solomon said, "It is better to have only a little, with peace of mind, than be busy all the time" (Eccl. 4:6, GNT). Sometimes, one of the healthiest things you can do for your life is to slow down. Maybe you're thinking, "Easy for you to say, Trav. But how would I do that?"

I get it. We're busy. Slowing down in a fast-paced society seems impossible. We live in a drag-race society. We want what we want and we want it now. We speed on the freeways and blow our horns and gaskets when people get in our way. We microwave our food and drive through restaurants because we've gotta keep racing. We want the fastest phones, fastest computers, and fastest Internet connections; and if they start to slow down, we will replace them. I believe we need rehab, because we are addicted to speed.

Setting the Pace

So when *is* the last time you took that chill pill? When is the last time you went stargazing, or watched the clouds drift by, watched the sunset, went fishing, or sat by a river and skipped rocks? For most of us, these are foreign concepts and few and far between. We are sprinting through life! But if you want to live a healthy life of rest and relaxation, remember that life is a marathon, not a sprint. You may need to reset the pace of your life.

Several years ago I had the privilege of doing the invocation for NASCAR at Phoenix International Raceway. It's pretty cool how NASCAR does this before every race. The chaplain or pastor walks onto the middle of the race track, in front of thousands of people in person and millions on television, and lifts up the name of Jesus and prays a prayer of safety and protection over the racers. Way to spread the gospel, NASCAR!

And as if that wasn't awesome enough, I was asked to jump in the pace car with the pace car driver before the race. As the pace car drove around the track, all of the race cars took their positions and followed behind. It was so cool! I felt like a real racer. It was an amazing feeling as the pace car cruised at eighty miles per hour around the track. You could hear the powerful roar of all the race-car engines revving up all around you. The pace car set the pace.

Let me ask you this question: What is setting the pace for your life? Your calendar? Your work schedule? Your desire to acquire? Your disease to people-please? If you set the pace of your life against anything other than God's pace for your life, it will leave you beat up, beat down, and burnt out. Allow God to set the pace for your life—not society, your job, your kids, or anything else except God. Paul said in Galatians 5:22 (NIV), "Since we live by the Spirit, let us keep in step with the Spirit." Allow God and only God to set the pace for your life and keep in step with the Spirit.

Creating Extra Space

Creating a healthy life isn't just about the pace, it's also about the space. This is called margin. We all need some margin in our lives. Let's face it, our lives are overcrowded. We have too many things going on—too many commitments, too many text messages, too much work, and too much debt. We are on overload. Instead of living life with some built-in reserve, we are living life with shattered nerves. What we need is some space. What we need is margin.

Maybe you've read about the Banqiao Dam on the River Ru in China. On August 5, 1975, a ferocious typhoon brought record rainstorms to the city. As the rains came down, the floods came up and the water levels in the area's rivers skyrocketed. The added pressure put enormous stress on the reservoirs, causing the smaller dams to burst and collapse like dominos. Eventually, all the pressure from the extreme weather conditions, the extra rainfall, and the water rushing in from broken dams built up and put so much pressure and distress on the dam that it too burst and collapsed. It's become known as the greatest dam failure in history. In fact, its failure caused more casualties than any other dam failure in history, with an estimated 171,000 casualties.

The dam wasn't designed nor built to handle the added stress and pressure from the extra water from the rainfall or the other collapsed dams. It needed margin. And so do you. If you don't have space and margin in your life, when the storms blow your way and batter you with the added stress and pressure, you will collapse.

You weren't designed to carry the weight of the world. You weren't created to take on the burden yourself. You weren't designed to live your life on overload. You need to allow God to set the pace, and you need to allow yourself some space.

Reflect for a moment on your life. How much space *do* you have in your life? Chances are, you don't have enough. Maybe you feel like Job when he said, "My days go by faster than a runner; they fly away without my seeing any joy" (Job 9:25, NCV). In his book *Margin*, Dr. Richard Swenson wrote this:

> The conditions of modern day living devour margin. If you're homeless we direct you to a shelter. If you're penniless we offer you food stamps. If you're breathless we connect you to oxygen. But if you're marginless we give you one more thing to do. Marginless is being thirty minutes late to the doctor's office because you were twenty minutes late getting out of the hairdresser because you were ten minutes late dropping the children off at school because the car ran out of gas two blocks from a gas station and you forgot your purse. That's marginless.

Margin, on the other hand, is having breath at the top of the staircase, money at the end of the month and sanity left over at the end of adolescence.

Marginless is the baby crying and the phone ringing at the same time. Margin is grandma taking the baby for the afternoon.

Marginless is being asked to carry a load five pounds heavier than you can lift. Margin is having a friend carry half the burden.

Marginless is not having time to finish the book you're reading on stress. Margin is having the time to read it twice.

Marginless is fatigue. Margin is energy.

Marginless is red ink. Margin is black ink.

Marginless is hurry. Margin is calm.

Marginless is our culture. Margin is counter-culture, having some space in your life and schedule.

Marginless is reality. Margin is remedy.

Marginless is the disease of our decade and margin is the cure.

(*Margin: Restoring Emotional, Physical, Financial, and Time Reserved to Overloaded Lives* [Colorado Springs: Nav-Press, 1992, 32).

I pray you'll make some space and margin in your life.

Rejuvenate

If you search the Internet or bookstore seeking tips on how to rejuvenate yourself, you'll find suggestions about products you can purchase, getting a spa treatment, working on breathing techniques, getting good exercise, or getting away. And although each of these are certainly powerful and beneficial for us to rejuvenate, the only way to truly rejuvenate is to tap into God's strength and power to recharge your life, *daily*. In fact, in Matthew 11:28–30 (NIV), Jesus outlines the three keys for total rejuvenation. Look what he said:

> "Come to me, all you who are weary and burdened, and I will give you rest. Take my yoke upon you and learn from me, for I am gentle and humble in heart, and you will find rest for your souls. For my yoke is easy and my burden is light."

Within these three verses, Jesus outlines the three keys for total rejuvenation:

1. **Come to Jesus.** Jesus said, "Come to me, all you who are weary and burdened, and I will give you rest." When you're tired, weak, and weary, instead of slamming more coffee or more energy drinks, go to Jesus. Get in God's presence. Pray, praise, worship, and read the Word. Tap into his power and he will give you rest and rejuvenate you.

   Coach Vince Lombardi said, "Fatigue makes cowards of us all." Without God's rejuvenating presence, life is not only tiring, but life is also scary. You never want to live a day of your life without the presence of God in your life; if you do, you're extremely vulnerable.

   Moses knew all about the importance of going to God and getting in his presence. He was well aware of the importance of having the presence of God in his life in order to stay rejuvenated, protected, and directed. In fact, Moses knew that without God's presence in his life, it was useless for him to even attempt anything. In Exodus 33:14 (NLT) God speaks to Moses: The Lord replied, "I will personally go with you, Moses, and I will give you rest—everything will be fine for you." It's as if God is saying, "No matter what kind of hell you may go through, Moses, heaven will be with you." In Exodus 33:15 (NIV), we see Moses respond. When he spoke face to face with the Lord, he said, "If your presence does not go with us, do not send us up from here." In other words, "God, if you go, I'll go!"

I know some of you reading this book are going through your own personal hell today. For some of you, you're about to lose your marriage. For some of you, you just lost a loved one. For some of you, you just got bad news from your doctor. For some of you, you just lost your job. The devil has been working overtime to wear you down, beat you down, and burden you down with all the pressures and hardships of life.

If you're going through hell today, remember that Jesus is with you. God is personally walking with you. You might be in the roughs of life, but you're going to come out shining like a diamond. You might be tried in the fire, but you're going to come out refined like gold. Jesus said, "Come to me, all you who are weary and burdened, and I will give you rest."

2. **Take Jesus' yoke.** The second key to rejuvenation Jesus mentions in Matthew 11 is, "Take my yoke upon you." What *is* he talking about? The word "yoke" that Jesus used is a farming term. A *yoke* is a bar of wood placed over the necks of two animals to unite and bind them for the purpose of them pulling together, working together, making them stronger as they share the load in the fields together. A yoke helps lighten the load. And Jesus is saying to you and me: Take a load off. Give it to me. I want to help you. You weren't designed to carry that weight, that burden, that stress on your own. Let me rejuvenate you. "Give all your worries and cares to God, for he cares about you" (1 Pet. 5:7, NLT). Come to Jesus, and take a load off.

3. **Learn from Jesus.** The third key Jesus gives us is this, "learn from me ... and you will find rest for your souls." Clearly,

Jesus weathered some storms and lived through incredible stress, pressure, and fatigue. As we read and study the Holy Scriptures, we can learn from Jesus. In fact, just before Jesus was betrayed and arrested, the Bible tells us he was suffering and in agony. And what did he do? He went to his father. He kneeled about and prayed and trusted God to provide his added strength.

> He walked away, about a stone's throw, and knelt down and prayed, "Father, if you are willing, please take this cup of suffering away from me. Yet I want your will to be done, not mine." Then an angel from heaven appeared and strengthened him. He prayed more fervently, and he was in such agony of spirit that his sweat fell to the ground like great drops of blood (Luke 22:41–44, NLT).

Today, if you are fatigued, tired, weary, and weak, go to Jesus and cast your burdens upon him. If you're beat up, beat down, and burdened with the stresses, pressures, and weights of this world, go to Jesus and take a load off. God never created you to carry the weight of the world.

Three Keys to Leaving the "BUT . . . I'm Too Tired" Excuse behind You

#1—Rest
Get some rest. Take that nap. Sleep at night. Rest in the presence of God. Remember the words of Jesus, "Come to me, and I will give you rest."

#2—Relax
Create some space and some margin and relax. Take a chill pill! Allow God to be the pacesetter for your life. Walk in step with the Spirit.

#3—Rejuvenate

My prayer for you is Romans 15:13 (NLT); it's a prayer of rejuvenation. And I have already prayed this for *you*: "I pray that God, the source of hope, will fill you completely with joy and peace because you trust in him. Then you will overflow with confident hope through the power of the Holy Spirit."

I encourage you to make it your prayer, too. Take and trust your burden to Jesus and allow him to carry your weight, so you can rejuvenate!

CHAPTER TEN

BUT . . . MY PAST

Just because we are products of our past doesn't mean we forfeit our future.

Forget about what's happened; don't keep going over old history. Be alert, be present. I'm about to do something brand-new. It's bursting out! Don't you see it? There it is! I'm making a road through the desert, rivers in the badlands.

Isaiah 43:18–19, MES

There's nothing more haunting and daunting than the *buts* of our past. I would, but, my past. I could, but, my past. If you're not careful, not only can your past stop you in your tracks, but it can also cause you to stray off the path. When you drive a car, it's extremely dangerous and even potentially fatal to drive down the road while constantly looking at your rear-view mirror. Likewise, it's extremely dangerous and even potentially fatal to live your life trying to move forward while constantly looking backward at your past. Our pasts can lead us through all sorts of excuses like, but, look what I've done; but, my reputation; but, I've been divorced; but, I've been in prison; but, I've been abused; but, the family I come from; but, but, but!

The fact is, we all have jacked-up pasts that have the ability to distract us or keep us locked up. But the good news is, God's Word is the liberating manual and mandate for our lives to move us *past our pasts* and to help us forge our futures! As screwed up as your past

129

may be, the cool thing is that it can propel you into a customized purpose for your future. Just because we are products of our past, doesn't mean we forfeit our future.

You're as Good as New

If you've been having a hard time moving past your past, I have a special word from God just for you. God wants to tell you this right now:

> Forget about what's happened; don't keep going over old history. Be alert, be present. I'm about to do something brand-new. It's bursting out! Don't you see it? There it is! I'm making a road through the desert, rivers in the badlands (Isa. 43:18–19, MES).

Isn't that exciting?! God is about to do something brand-new, in *you*. It's bursting out! He's making a road though the desert *just for you*. I don't know about you, but these two verses get me pumped up. I love those words *brand-new*! I'm thankful that God is a God of new beginnings, fresh starts, and do-overs. The Bible has so much to say about new beginnings and starting over! Check out just a few of these life-changing scriptures about new beginnings—one for every day of the week:

- Therefore, if anyone is in Christ, he is a new creation. The old has passed away; behold, the new has come (2 Cor. 5:17, ESV).

- Everything—and I do mean everything—connected with that old way of life has to go. It's rotten through and through. Get rid of it! And then take on an entirely new way of life—a God-fashioned life, a life renewed from the inside and working itself into your conduct as God accurately reproduces his character in you (Eph.4:22–24, MES).

- And I will give you a new heart, and a new spirit I will put within you. And I will remove the heart of stone from your flesh and give you a heart of flesh (Ezek. 36:26, ESV).

- Brothers, I do not consider that I have made it my own. But one thing I do: forgetting what lies behind and straining forward to what lies ahead (Phil. 3:13, ESV).

- As far as the east is from the west, so far has he removed our transgressions from us (Ps. 103:12, NIV).

- Once again you will have compassion on us. You will trample our sins under your feet and throw them into the depths of the ocean (Mic. 7:19, NLT).

- I'll forever wipe the slate clean of their sins (Heb. 10:17, MES).

Tell me those verses aren't incredible! God is a god of fresh starts and new beginnings. When you come to God, he says, "Out with the old, and in with the new." And that's why your past can never become the *but* that keeps you from moving forward.

No Turning Back

Often the biggest problem with us moving past our past has nothing to do with God and everything to do with us. It seems that we humans possess this natural ability to dwell on the past and use our minds like a constant instant replay. We keep looking back at our past over and over again like a broken record. But the Bible tells us not to look back.

Remember what happened to Lot's wife when she looked back? Genesis 19 tells us the crazy story about the destruction of Sodom and Gomorrah. Abraham had a nephew, Lot, who lived in Sodom with his family. As the story unfolds, two angels paid Lot a visit, and informed him and his family to get the heck out of town before God destroyed the entire city. Lot's family was warned, "Escape for your life! Do not look behind you, and do not stay anywhere in the valley; escape to the mountains, or you will be swept away" (Gen. 19:17, NIV). So Lot and his daughters listened and ran for their lives. "But his wife, from behind him, looked back, and she became a pillar of salt" (Gen. 19:26, NIV).

Sounds painful, doesn't it? Not really the way I wanna go out! She looked back and became a pillar of salt. Looking back not only stopped her in tracks and demobilized her from moving forward, but it took her life. Lot's wife lagged behind. She turned around and looked back. It's interesting because the Hebrew word for "looked back" means "to glance over one's shoulder, to regard, to consider, to pay attention to." What was she considering? What was she paying attention to? The Bible doesn't reveal what she was looking back toward, but perhaps as she turned and watched the flames consume her old life and everything she's ever had and valued, maybe she was thinking about the people and possessions of her past. I don't know. But we do know that it consumed her.

What about you? What do you keep looking back at? What are you considering or paying attention to?

It Has to Go

We humans are funny, aren't we? We want *God* to do something new; but *we* want to keep doing the same old things. Many people want a fresh start in life, but they also want to drag parts of their old rotten and stale lives into their new beginning. That's impossible! It all has to go!

I heard about a guy who wanted something new in life, so he gave up his long career to become a taxi driver. One day as he was driving for his new job, a guy in the back seat reached up and tapped the driver on the shoulder to ask him a question. The cab driver freaked! He lost control of the car, went up the sidewalk, and skidded off the road. They were both okay, and after a moment of relief and silence the driver turned and said, "Man, don't ever do that again! You scared the mess out of me!"

The passenger was confused and said, "I'm sorry, but I didn't realize that a little tap on the shoulder would scare you so much."

The driver replied, "Oh, I'm sorry, it's not really your fault. Today is my first day as a cab driver. For the past twenty-five years, I've been driving a funeral hearse."

My point is, we want God to do something new, but we try to drag our old ways into God's new ways and it can't be done. Let's look at Ephesians 4:22-24 (MSG) again: "everything—and I do mean everything—connected with that old way of life has to go. It's rotten through and through. Get rid of it! And then take on an entirely new way of life—a God-fashioned life, a life renewed from the inside and working itself into your conduct as God accurately reproduces his character in you." God's promises are true, he wants to start a brand-new you, but that also means that you've got to get rid of everything connected with your old way of life. And I do mean *everything* has to go!

Think about it for a minute. What are the things from your past that you need to stop looking at and going back to in order to move forward? They have to go! Moving past your past is going to consist of taking several different practical yet spiritual steps, action steps for your life. Since God is creating a new you, it's time to for you to say out with the old and in with the new!

Have you ever witnessed a dog throwing up and then eating its own vomit? I have. It's disgusting. I have a dog, Rocko, and I've seen Rocko eat all kinds of crap, literally. I'm sorry for the visual, but King Solomon in Proverbs drives home a nauseating yet perfectly well-put illustration when he says: "As a dog returns to its vomit, so a fool repeats his foolishness" (Prov. 26:11, NLT).

Much of our past *is* foolish and disgusting. So don't return to your vomit. The only way you're going to be able to truly move forward is to cut loose those things from your past that are trying to drag you down and keep you distant from Jesus. In some cases, your past may not even be a horrible, devastating, or sinful event;

it might simply be something that keeps you from moving toward God and forward *with* God.

Jesus, the Master Sermonator, broke it down for us about the cost of following him, the importance of throwing off the dead weight in our lives, and the importance of never looking back. We looked at a portion of these words from Jesus a bit earlier, but let's look at them again, in a little more depth:

> As they were walking along, someone said to Jesus, "I will follow you wherever you go." But Jesus replied, "Foxes have dens to live in, and birds have nests, but the Son of Man has no place even to lay his head." He said to another person, "Come, follow me." The man agreed, but he said, "Lord, first let me return home and bury my father." But Jesus told him, "Let the spiritually dead bury their own dead! Your duty is to go and preach about the Kingdom of God." Another said, "Yes, Lord, I will follow you, but first let me say good-bye to my family." But Jesus told him, "Anyone who puts a hand to the plow and then looks back is not fit for the Kingdom of God." (Luke 9:57–62, NLT)

But First

Did you notice the *buts* these potential disciples had? "I will follow you wherever you go…*but first*, let me return home and bury my father. … *But first* let me say good-bye to my family." Jesus' response is unimaginable: "Let the dead bury their own dead. Anyone who puts a hand to the plow and then looks back is not fit for the Kingdom of God." Sounds harsh, doesn't it? It does to me, too.

But that's exactly the point. The cost of following Jesus is no joke. In fact, it's going to cost you everything you've got. You can't ride the fence and be half-in and half-out. You can't even be ninety-nine percent in and one percent out. It's all or nothing, baby. God doesn't want part of you; he wants *every* part of you. Jesus said, "If anyone would come after me, let him deny himself and take up his cross and follow me. For whoever would save his life will lose it, but whoever loses his life for my sake will find it. For what will it profit a man if he gains the whole world and forfeits his soul? Or what shall a man give in return for his soul?" (Matt.16:24–26, NIV).

The sad truth is, we all have a bunch of *but first* excuses to put Jesus off, too. As humans, we all have a fatal flaw; we have attractions to distractions. We say we love God, and we do. But the attractions to distractions prevent us from truly being "all in." As Jesus said, "The attractions of this world, the delights of wealth, the search for success and lure of nice things come in and crowd out God" (Mark 4:19, LB). We have good intention, but bad attention. We offer Jesus a bunch of lip service instead of life service. It's nothing new to Jesus. People have been living their lives like this since Adam and Eve. In fact, as Jesus was talking to (and about) the Pharisees, he quoted a verse from Isaiah 29:13, written seven hundred years before Christ: "These people honor me with their lips, but their hearts are far from me" (Matt. 15:18, NIV). It's the *but first* syndrome. I will follow you Jesus, *but first* I wanna live for me. I will start tithing, *but first* I need to get a raise or pay off some bills. I will get involved in my church, *but first* let me get through this season of my life. I will go on that mission trip, but first. … God, I'm all yours, *but first*!

You Assume What You Consume

It's impossible to be totally consumed by Jesus when we are constantly consuming the things of this world. If you want to be all in for Jesus, you'll need to change your diet. The saying is true: You are what you eat, physically, spiritually, emotionally, and socially. What are you feeding your body, mind, and spirit?

I heard a story about a lady who noticed an old, happy man sitting on his porch. "Excuse me," she said, "Sir, I just couldn't help but notice how happy you look. And you look so young! Tell me, what is the secret to your long, happy life?"

"Well," the man responded, "I eat fatty foods and never exercise. I also smoke three packs of cigarettes a day, and drink about a case of whiskey a week!"

The woman said, "Wow! And how old are you?"

"Twenty-eight."

Funny, yet not-so-funny, because you are what you eat. Let me give you a little secret to life: The character you consume will become the character you assume. Therefore, I encourage you to do some self-evaluation. Pay careful attention to your consumption. What and whom do you listen to?

Losing Is Finding

Losing is finding. It's addition by subtraction. It defies logical thinking. When I lose something, I want to find it. I will work tirelessly scouring the house to find whatever it is I lost. But as Jesus said, "whoever loses his life for my sake will find it." You found life by losing life. Finding Christ meant, and continues to mean, losing yourself to him and in him. What does that mean? What are we losing? You're losing the old sinful you and your old way of life that's rotten through and through. I'm losing the old, sinful Travis. My sins, my patterns of sins, my sinful habits, my sinful nature, the way I think, my attitude, my pride, my insecurities, and my ego—I lose them all. And I don't return to my vomit.

Lose your life for Christ's sake and you will find it. John the Baptist put it like this, "He must increase, but I must decrease" (John 3:30, ESV). More of you, God! And less of me!

For some of you, one of the toughest parts of losing your life for Jesus will be losing some old friends who are pulling you down from your walk with God. Instead, you need friends who will push you toward him. No buts, no excuses! Paul said, "Do not be misled: 'Bad company corrupts good character.'" (1 Cor. 15:33, NIV). The bottom line is: A friend with bad character will make *you* a friend with bad character. I'm not saying you shouldn't be casual friends with someone. What I am saying is that you shouldn't be close friends with everybody. I'm convinced that the friends you choose are the number-one influencing factor in how close or how distant your relationship with God is. Your friends are either helping you or they're hurting you. They're pulling you and Jesus apart, or pushing you and Jesus together.

Even good friends whom you love dearly can lead you astray. When I was five, I was at my best friend Matthew's house, a couple of houses down the road from ours. We played and played and then went to the kitchen for some snacks. There was a clothing iron sitting on their kitchen table. Matthew said to me, "I dare you to put your hand on that iron." Some best friend, right? But boy, do I love a good dare!

However, I responded, "No way—my mom said those things are hot and that will hurt bad. I'm not touching that thing."

He said, "Nah, it won't hurt; your mom is just telling you that so you don't mess with it." He continued, "Besides, it's not even plugged in, look!"

I looked down under the table, and sure enough, I saw a power cable just dangling down below. So, I walked over and smashed the entire palm of my hand against the iron and burned the hot mess out of it! It *was* plugged in and I *was* an idiot! Apparently, I had noticed a different cord dangling.

My point is, your friends have influence over you. They can either hurt you or they can help you. Choose your close friends prayerfully and carefully. The Bible has a lot to say about the kinds of friends we are to choose. Here's just a few examples from the book of Proverbs:

- As iron sharpens iron, so one person sharpens another (Prov. 27:17, NIV).
- A mirror reflects a man's face but what he is really like is shown by the kind of friends he chooses (Prov. 27:19, GNT).

- A righteous man is cautious in friendships (Prov. 12:26, NIV).

- He who walks with the wise grows wise (Prov. 13:20, NIV).

In fact, Proverbs details sixteen types of people we should not be close friends with, including lazy people, immoral people, angry people, greedy people, and unbelieving people. The point I'm trying to make is that you have to choose friends prayerfully and carefully. Not everyone that walks into your life is supposed to be a close friend. Choose friends who fly and soar at higher heights—people who have higher standards, higher morals, higher goals, higher convictions, higher expectations. God created eagles to soar in the sky, and God created you to soar in the sky. Be an eagle Christian. Set your eyes on things above, and soar at higher heights for your life.

Too many Christians are chicken Christians. You know what chicken Christians are like? Chicken Christians are afraid of everything. Afraid to share their faith. Afraid to pray publicly. They love to follow other chickens. Chickens go with the flow. Chickens could care less about the things above. They're content with the chicken coop and chicken crap on the ground. They're always scratching the dirt, looking for food, looking down at the ground. They're earthbound and they don't fly long distances, even though they could.

Chickens are also kind of like sheep. Jesus referred to us as sheep and it wasn't a compliment. Sheep are dumb. Sheep just follow the butts in front of them. They don't ask questions; they just go with the flow. Sheep have knees, but they don't use them. They just walk around straight-legged. Baaaaaa. Baaaaaa.

Sadly, too many Christians are just like that. They spend all their time following and conforming. They could soar, but for some reason they'd rather be walking around in crap. Listen, here's a tip for you: It's hard to soar like an eagle when you're surrounded by chickens and sheep. Get some new friends. Out with the old and in with the new!

God wants everything. All of it. God wants to say to you, "No more *but firsts*, and no more excuses." God gave up his life for yours. Will you give your life for his? It's time. The time is now, like never before, to press forward and never look back! It's time to cut the ties and throw off the dead weight in your life. They're dragging you down. And ultimately, they're corrupting your life with Christ.

Total Surrender

Years ago, our neighbor's house was broken into. It was crazy. She was a widow and as she pulled up into her garage, two dudes with beanies covering their faces ran out of the garage, jumped in their car, and fled the scene. She later discovered that approximately fifteen thousand dollars in belongings had been stolen. A few days later, around 9 p.m., I was outside in my backyard holding a flashlight while I readjusted the timer to our irrigation sprinkler system. As I continued working on the timer for quite some time, I suddenly heard what I thought to be footsteps in my front yard. With the burglary fresh in my mind, I carefully walked toward the front of the yard. Sure enough, there were intruders in my yard!

As I shined my flashlight directly at the men, I heard a loud booming voice shout, "Police! Drop your flashlight and put your hands in the air!" They had their hands on their guns and police dogs on leashes, and they were staring at me!

I surrendered! In fact, the hair on the back of my neck stood up and surrendered! I immediately dropped my flashlight and threw my hands in the air as the officer shouted, "What are you doing back there?"

"Fixing my irrigation system, sir."

He said sarcastically, "You live here, huh?"

"Yes sir, I do."

"You got some identification?"

I replied, "Yes, but I will have to go into my house to get it." We talked for a bit afterward, and I learned that my recently burglarized neighbor called the cops on me, as she thought she saw a burglar in my backyard.

This taught me a great lesson on what true surrender looks like. Total surrender is dropping everything and throwing your hands up in the air toward Jesus. Total surrender is saying, "God, I'm yours. I'm holding nothing. I'm keeping nothing. And I'm hiding nothing." Total surrender is not just lip service; it's life service. God wants total surrender, not a total pretender. Total surrender is what Jesus modeled for you when he died on the cross for you because of his love for you.

Look, God is after you. He's chasing you. And guess what? He's faster than you. You can't outrun God. You can run as fast as you can around the corners of life and he's there, too! And he will never stop chasing you and never stop running after you because he will never stop loving you. God loves you so much that he gave his one and only Son to die for you so that you can truly live!

The Zimbabwe Way

My good friend Albert Mavunga lives in Zimbabwe, Africa. Albert is engaged to a girl named Faith, who also lives in Zimbabwe. Several months ago, before Albert had proposed to Faith, I asked him when he thought the wedding would be. He told me, "I don't know. Before I can propose to Faith, I have to get her parents' permission and offer them cash and cows."

I replied with something like, "Wait, what? Cash and cows?" I thought he was joking.

He said, "Yes, it's custom in Africa. It is the Zimbabwe Way. I have to ask the parents' permission to marry her, and I have to offer a certain amount of cash and cows when I ask them. So I'm going to offer five thousand dollars and five cows."

I said, "Really? What happens if your cash-and-cow offer isn't enough?"

Albert said, "Then you're in debt. The parents tell you what their daughter is worth, and if she's worth more than the amount of cash and cows you offered, and you still want to marry your lady, you're in debt to the parents. You can marry her, but you will be in debt to the parents until they are paid off."

Interesting, right? I told him he needs to find a good American girl because her parents will actually pay *him* to take her by paying for the wedding!

As strange as this story seems, the Zimbabwe Way mirrors some deep spiritual concepts of the Bible. Love costs dearly and true love comes with a price. You can give without loving, but you cannot love without giving. And Jesus loves you so much that he gave up his life for yours. There is no greater love than that. Jesus said: "Greater love has no one than this, that someone lay down his life for his friends" (John 15:13, ESV). Paul adds, "You were bought with a price. So glorify God in your body" (1 Cor. 6:20, ESV).

And this is where the rubber meets the road about your past. It's been paid for. Jesus paid the price for your sins by being nailed to the cross. Your past has been paid for and purchased by the blood of Jesus because God loves you. "For God so loved the world that he gave his one and only Son that whoever believes in him shall not perish but have everlasting life" (John 3:16, NIV). Let me tell you something, that's a lot of love! Do you know how much love you'd have to have in your heart to give your child's life away for someone else's life?

Let me paint the picture a little bit. Josiah is my one and only son. He's twelve. He's my man, my little dude, my homie, and I love him dearly. But let's imagine we're all sitting in church and a guy walks up in the middle of service with a gun and starts screaming and yelling like a lunatic that he's going to kill all of you. I start pleading with the guy, "No, please don't. Please don't. I'm begging you not to. Just tell me what you want. I'll do anything." And he says, "Okay, it's your choice. You give me your son and I'll take him or it's everyone else sitting here." I've got news for you: You're all going to be with Jesus a lot sooner than you thought! I mean, I love you guys, but that's my son, my one and only son. Who would give their son away for the sake of others?

God would, that's who. And God did. Because that's how much he loves us.

And that's what this entire book is all about: God's unconditional love for you. God loves you, unconditionally, in spite of you. God looked past your past before you even entered your past. There's nothing you've done, and nothing you can do, to separate yourself from God's love. As the apostle Paul said, "I am convinced that nothing can ever separate us from God's love. Neither death nor life, neither angels nor demons, neither our fears for today nor our worries about tomorrow—not even the powers of hell can separate us from God's love. No power in the sky above or in the earth below—indeed, nothing in all creation will ever be able to separate us from the love of God that is revealed in Christ Jesus our Lord" (Rom. 8:38–39, NLT).

Infected or Infectious

You have a past and so do I. We've all been infected by the disease of our pasts. Now you have a choice: Be infected, or become infectious. Moving past your past is not just about you and your eternal life, but also about other people and your earthly life. God wants to use you. God wants to use your past to help others with their future. Will you let him? I'm not suggesting that you need to broadcast your junk to the entire world. What I *am* saying is that God wants you to use your life, past, present, and future to point others toward him.

If you had the cure for cancer, would you share it with the world or keep it to yourself? Of course you'd share it. To withhold such a breakthrough would be the most selfish thing in the world you could do. There is a disease far worse than cancer and that is the disease of sin and self. And you have the cure: Jesus Christ. Will you share it? Be infectious!

Final Words

If you've ever experienced the deeply moving moments of listening to the final words of a loved one just before they passed on, you have a real blessing. The final words of a loved one are rich with emotion and rich with significance. They hold enormous weight and importance to us. What would you say to your loved ones if you knew they'd be the final words before you breathed your last breath?

In Matthew 28, we were given the final words of Jesus after his resurrection and before he left earth. What were his final words? They must have been incredibly important and intentional. These final words are known as the Great Commission, and here they are:

> Therefore, go and make disciples of all the nations, baptizing them in the name of the Father and the Son and the Holy Spirit. Teach these new disciples to obey all the commands I have given you. And be sure of this: I am with you always, even to the end of the age (Matt. 28:19–20, NLT).

The final words of Jesus to us reveal his purpose for our life: to reach people for Jesus and teach people about Jesus. He leaves us with a mandate, a commission and a call to action, "go and make disciples of all the nations." And that is exactly what his disciples did with their lives, and that is exactly what he wants you to do with your life. It's called the Great Commission, not the Great Omission or Great Suggestion. We are *commissioned*. Go. Reach and teach for Jesus. You have the answer to all of life's problems—Jesus. Will you share him?

Let Your Light Shine

Now let's flip the script for a minute and rewind. In Matthew 5, we find the most famous sermon Jesus ever preached, the Sermon on the Mount. What would he preach about? Much like his final words, these words would be important. What would you preach about? Of course, Jesus, but in what context? His death and resurrection? Love? Grace? Forgiveness? Pride? Sin?

Jesus came out strong and told us to live out our faith. He opens with eight attitudes we should all possess, and then in verse 14–16 (NIV) he says this:

> You are the light of the world. A town built on a hill cannot be hidden. Neither do people light a lamp and put it under a bowl. Instead they put it on its stand, and it gives light to everyone in the house. In the same way, let your light shine before others, that they may see your good deeds and glorify your Father in heaven.

Let your light shine. Live your faith. He's not saying stand on a street corner and hold up a sign that says, "Stop Your Sin, Let Jesus in," "Turn or Burn," or "Get Right or Get Left Behind." (Hey, I've seen people do this.) What he *is* saying is this: Live out your faith. Let your light shine. You don't have to shine your light *and* beat people over the head with your Bible, simply *let your light shine.* Be true. Be a man or woman of God. Don't just talk the talk, walk the walk.

Sure, there will be times when you get to share your story or share the Word of God, but as Francis of Assisi said, "Preach the gospel at all times, and when necessary use words." Your life is a sermon being read and listened to each and every day of your life. Be a Matthew 5 sermon for people. Possess the attitudes, character, and integrity of Jesus, and let your light shine so people will see Jesus!

And when you do have an opportunity to share Christ verbally, you can always start with your testimony. The most powerful tool you have for sharing Jesus is your own life story. It's hard to argue with testimony. No one can debate what God has done in your heart and in your life. God gave you the stories of your past, stories of how he brought you through, to share and to help people with their future.

Be bold and unashamed. Jesus said, "Neither do people light a lamp and put it under a bowl." Christians aren't supposed to blend into the world; they're supposed to set the trend for the world. Be a trendsetter! I dare you—no, I double-dog dare you with a back flip—to light up your light and live your life ablaze for Jesus Christ. When something's on fire, people take notice. Be bold and unashamed!

Mark Twain said, "Be bold and never be afraid to go out on a limb; that's where the fruit is." Live your life unashamed and unapologetic for the sake of Jesus Christ. Let Romans 1:16 (NIV) be one of the theme verses for your life, "For I am not ashamed of the gospel, because it is the power of God that brings salvation to everyone who believes."

God has done his part. Now it's time for you to do your part. He's moved past your past, and now it's time for *you* to move past your past. Today is a brand-new day! Today is chapter one, page one in the brand new story being written for the rest of your life. So get off your *buts* and write it!

Four Keys to Leaving the "BUT . . . My Past" Excuse behind You

#1—Forget What's Behind

Now is the time to move onward and upward. Remember God's Word for you. (And if you don't, review the verses earlier in this chapter.) Don't keep going over old history; God's about to do something brand-new in you! I hope that penetrates and resonates deep within your soul.

God, we claim Isaiah 43:18–19 for our lives: "Forget about what's happened; don't keep going over old history. Be alert, be present. I'm about to do something brand-new. It's bursting out! Don't you see it? There it is! I'm making a road through the desert, rivers in the badlands."

#2—Forge toward the Future

Forget what is behind, forge toward the future, as we remember the words of the apostle Paul: "But one thing I do: forgetting what lies behind ... and straining forward to what lies ahead. ..."

146 Your BUT'S Too Big

Remember, your future is not just about you, but about everyone else around you. You have the cure. You have the answer. It's time to share it!

#3 Focus on Your Mission

Populate heaven! Make this your prayer: "God, I pray that because of my love for you and my life for you, more people will go to heaven when they die and less people go through hell while they live." Lose your life for Jesus' sake and you will find it. Give your life for the sake of Jesus Christ; after all, he gave his life for yours. Keep your focus on your mission—the Great Commission. Reach people for Jesus and teach people about Jesus. God wants to use you. Love the Lord your God with all your heart, all your soul, and all your mind, and love your neighbor as yourself (Matt. 22:37-39).

#4—Finish Strong

Paul said, "I have fought the good fight, I have finished the race, I have kept the faith" (2 Tim. 4:7, ESV). I pray those words will be the words you will say at the end of your life. Finish strong. Keep your eyes on Jesus and never look back. Don't become a tumbleweed Christian, uprooted and blown around by the winds of life. Be deeply rooted in Jesus Christ and finish strong. Forget the past, forge toward the future, focus on your mission, and finish strong. *No buts. No excuses.*

ACKNOWLEDGMENTS

You

First and foremost, I would like to thank you for investing your time into reading this book. I pray this book is a motivational, inspirational, and transformational weapon for you to move past your excuses and into your dreams! It is my dream that this book will light a fire within the depths of your soul to step out and live your dream.

My Wife, Natalie

Thank you to my wife Natalie. You always stand by my side praying for me and championing me all along the ways of my God-given dreams. I am a greater man of God because of you. Thank you for being the anchor of my life and the anchor of our family. You are my best friend, soulmate, partner in Christ. I am madly in love with you and forever grateful that God brought you into my life.

My kiddos, Kylie, Josiah, and Jazzlyn

Thank you guys for being such awesome kids! You are my joy. God gave me the most amazing and special gifts imaginable when he gave me the three of you. I couldn't be more proud of each one of you. Even at your young ages, you are anointed by God and relentlessly dedicated to his work. You are so driven and motivated in all the things you put your minds to that you inspire me to move past my own excuses! I love you.

My Mom, Toni

Thank you for raising me to never believe anything less than what God's Word says in Philippians 4:13 (NKJV), "I can do all things through Christ who gives me strength." You are the biblical model of what it looks like to be tried in the fire and come out shining like gold. Thank you for your never-ending prayers and intercession, and thank you for exemplifying unconditional love. I love you.

My Church, Impact Church

I am proud of you and I am proud to call you family. You always rise to the call for the Great Commission and the Great Commandment. My family and I cherish each and every moment we spend with you and we are incredibly excited about God's plans for your future. You are champions for Christ. Never stop making an impact!

Two of My Mentors and Pastors, Rick Warren and David Chrzan

It would be impossible to articulate how thankful and grateful I am for both of you. It seems as if there isn't a week that goes by that either I or my staff doesn't call you or one of your staff. You two, along with the Saddleback Church staff, are the perfect model of what a selfless church looks like. Thank you for investing in me, my family, and my church. And thank you for being my pastors.

My Agent, David Shepherd

Thank you, David, for continuing your excellent work with me on our second project together. You are godly, professional, knowledgeable, and an extremely hard worker. I look forward to many years together in future projects and pray God's continued blessing on your family and ministry. May God richly bless you!

Deep River Books

Thank you Bill Carmichael and the Deep River team for investing in this project and making this dream a reality. You have a high character, and a godly and professional team that makes the book-writing process a complete joy. I am thankful for you!

My Lord and Savior

I dedicate this book to you, Jesus. Because, "with you, all things are possible." There is no excuse that I could ever dream up that you won't help me overcome. You are the ultimate motivator and encourager. You have given me second chance after second chance. You have believed in me even though I haven't believed in me. You have taught me what it means to finish strong, no matter what it might cost. I love you, Jesus.

ABOUT THE AUTHOR

 Travis Hearn is senior pastor of Impact Church in Scottsdale, Arizona—one of the fastest growing churches in the nation. He serves as team chaplain to the Phoenix Suns and has served as a Major League Baseball chaplain for over a decade. Travis lives in the Phoenix Metro area with his wife, Natalie, and their three children.

Also by Travis Hearn: *Game Changer: The Defining Moment That Takes You From Trials to Triumph.*

Please visit TravisHearn.com
Follow Travis on Twitter and Instagram @TravisHearn